# Joy of Hooking

## (With Yarn!)

Lenore is modeling a gorgeous antique hooked rug,
ca. 1950, 9'x5' wool yarn on cotton

## by Judy Taylor

2

(opposite) Twillingate Long Point Lighthouse, designed by Joan Foster, hooked by Ruth Elliot, 25"x32" wool yarn on burlap

## Acknowledgements

Tremendous thanks to the many artists who contributed to this book:

Rosemary Thomas, Kanata, Ontario
Pam Langdon, Ottawa, Ontario
Bonnie Campbell, Nepean, Ontario
Stephanie Ellyas, Sequim, Washington
Nancy Forsman, Bloomington, Minnesota
Sigrid Grant, Ottawa, Ontario
Patti Finch, Marmora, Ontario
Dianne Warren, St. John's, Newfoundland
Kerry MacPhail, Bellevue, Washington
Linda Rehlinger, Qualicum, British Columbia
Jill Purcell, Campbellford, Ontario
Teresa Waldo, Auburn, Washington
Cole Adams, Maple Valley, Washington
Gail Sherman Feetham, Timberlea, Nova Scotia
Tina Stewart, Corner Brook, Newfoundland
Cherie Langlois, Kapowsin, Washington
Anne Woodall, Kingston, Ontario
Andrea Hammel, Perth, Ontario
Michele LeBlanc, Hillsboro, Oregon
Dianne Cross, Sidney, British Columbia
Ruth Elliot, Lewisporte, Newfoundland
Susie Wilson, Canby, Oregon
Venissa Fancy, Lewisporte, Newfoundland
Janette Lambert, Gander, Newfoundland
Betty Pennell, Little Burnt Bay, Newfoundland
Joan Foster, Springdale, Newfoundland
Lyle Gowing, Otis, Oregon
Doreen Garrod, Edgewood, Washington
Maya Drummond, Londonderry, Vermont
Steve Grappe, San Angelo, Texas
Andrea Rheinlander, Sterling Heights, Michigan
Ellen Burleson, Canyon Lake, Texas

Yvonne MacLean, Hubbards, Nova Scotia
Crystal Morash, Hubbards, Nova Scotia
Colleen Taylor, Seattle, Washington
Paula Bowden, Yerington, Nevada
Khalil Zamini, Timonium, Maryland
Pat Ford, Seattle, Washington
Chris Searfoss, Port Charlotte, Florida
Linda and Allen Rosen, Linda Rosen Antiques, Sheffield, Massachusetts
Gary Taylor, Auburn, Washington
Lauren Perry, Seattle, Washington

And to Hugh and Suzanne Conrod, Hooked Rug Museum of North America, Chester Nova Scotia

Outport House, designed by Alice Kelly and Betty Pennell, hooked by Betty Pennell, 20"x30" wool yarn on burlap.

Please note: Ms. Taylor is a trained professional. Please do not attempt cockatiel wrangling at home.

Judy Taylor is an artist and farmer, rug hooker, hand spinner, and all around wool enthusiast from the beautiful Green River Valley in Washington State. Her first book, "Hooking With Yarn," sold out its initial printing. Her DVD, "A Beginners Guide to Traditional Nantucket Rug Hooking" won the Gold Award for Excellence at the ITVA Emerald City Awards, 1997. Many of her finished rugs, kits and patterns can be viewed at www.littlehouserugs.com.

Published by Little House Rugs
PO Box 2003
Auburn, Washington, 98071
© Copyright 2011 All rights reserved.
ISBN 978-0-615-51465-9
www.littlehouserugs.com

Bird of Paradise, designed and hooked by Judy Taylor, 27.5"x55.5" handspun and commercial yarn on linen.

# Contents

Introduction p. 7

Chapter 1
     What is Rug Hooking?  p. 9

Chapter 2
     Sundries You'll need to Hook with Yarn p. 17

Chapter 3
     Learning to Hook p. 23

Chapter 4
     Gallery p. 39

Chapter 5
     Project 1, Teddy Bear p. 67

Chapter 6
     Project 2, Dutch Treat p. 77

Chapter 7
     Project 3, Celtic Interlace Mat p. 81

Chapter 8
     Project 4, Waste Not Want Not Rug p. 89

Chapter 9
     Making your own Spiffy Rug Hooking Frame p. 97

Chapter 5
     Yarn hooking- Past, Present and Future p. 101

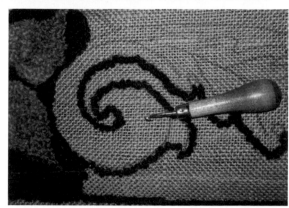

Bilbo Rug, designed and hooked by Judy Taylor, 48" round, Ewenique yarn on linen.

# Introduction

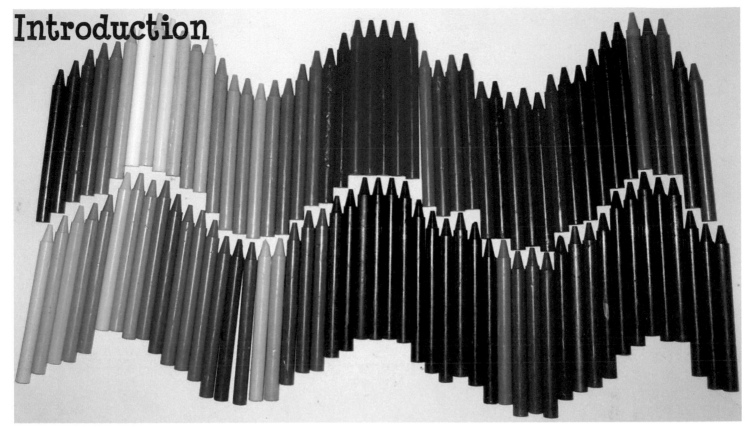

Remember crayons? Think about how much fun it was to color with crayons. As a child, you could easily wile away hours coloring. There was no limit to what you could do with crayons and your imagination.

You didn't even need a coloring book (although they were always fun too!), a blank piece of paper and a few crayons were all you needed to create beautiful pictures. When you opened up a brand new box of crayons- wow, what possibilities! And all those colors! They just cried out "Use me first! Use me first!" Just like Harold and his proverbial crayon, the whole wide world was there for you to explore and create.

Unfortunately, most of us grew up and forgot all about crayons. We moved on to more complex activities, like math, driving cars, getting jobs and doing our taxes. But we never lost the yearning to create, so we seek out "grown-up" crafts like rug hooking to satisfy that life-long desire to make things with our hands. But being "grownups," we so often question our abilities. How many times have we told ourselves "I can't draw" or "I need help with colors"?

When I hear these remarks from my students, I mention coloring with crayons, and some of that self-criticism melts away. When we were kids, we reveled in colors, doodling out designs for the sheer joy of feeling the wax rubbing on the paper, and the colors came alive in our hands. Rug hooking is just like coloring with crayons, only we color with yarn.

Father's Day Rug, 21"x30", designed by Colleen (age 6) and Gwendolyn (age 7), hooked by Judy Taylor, wool yarn on linen

Rug hooking is as versatile as a box of crayons. You're "coloring" with a child's freedom and creativity, but you're making "grownup" works of art that you can treasure for years.

Crown of Thorns close up, simple geometric design

You can hook rugs, pillows, stuffed animals, wall-hangings, stair runners, and more. You can hook in easy designs like geometrics (quilt patterns are a great beginner project!) or use realistic shading with elegant flowers and scrolls. No matter what style or design, the process of rug hooking is always the same; one loop at a time, pulled through a backing fabric like burlap or linen. The tool, a modified crochet hook, couldn't be simpler.

Antique Flower close up, complex shading design

In this book, you will learn the basics of this delightful craft. With clear instructions and four easy beginner projects, you will again be able to unlock your creativity using yarn as your medium (which sounds much more "grownup" after all).

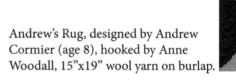

Andrew's Rug, designed by Andrew Cormier (age 8), hooked by Anne Woodall, 15"x19" wool yarn on burlap.

Just remember, if you can color it with crayons, you can hook it into a rug.

# Chapter 1

# What Is Rug Hooking?

Photo by Cherie Langlois

Grandma Guier's Rug, designed and hooked by Julia Wicker Guier, 38"x38"  wool yarn, ca. late 1800's

Rug hooking is a centuries-old craft, which enjoyed its real heyday in North America with the infusion of European settlement in the 1700's. Like so many home crafts carried over by these settlers, rug hooking is rooted in practicality. In the 18th Century anyone needing to make a rug could have devised a simple hook from a bent nail mounted in a handle, which would have been so small and easy to pack, it would have been ideal for people who needed to travel light. In those days yarn was a common product of any household, and worn-out woolen material was far too valuable to throw away, so these things were hooked into cozy rugs to warm the floors of these pioneer homes.

Lion with Palm Trees, ca. late 19th century, 67"x37" wool yarn. Courtesy of Linda Rosen Antiques

Folk Art Rug, ca. 1900, 2'x3' wool yarn. Courtesy of Khalil Zamini

There are many styles of rug hooking, all of which produce generally similar results. There is so called Traditional Rug Hooking, using cut strips of wool fabric, punch hooking, and (for want of a better term) Nantucket rug hooking, the type covered in this book. All three styles are "traditional," meaning that they all date back many hundreds of years. All produce beautiful rugs that last generations.

The earliest rugs were often quite simple in design, hooked in colors that could be created using natural dyes. They could be whimsical, even primitive, but always absolutely unique to the individuals who hooked them. That emptied feed sack was really an ideal blank canvas, and early rug hookers couldn't resist the urge to make up delightful pictures drawn from their experience and imagination. Rug hooking is a practical craft, yes, but it has always been a tremendous outlet for creativity.

Traditional and Nantucket styles both use the same rug hook, and the same backings. In each style, the loops are pulled from the back to the front, but the hooking technique differs between yarn and fabric strips, in order to take full advantage of the fiber used. In punch hooking, the yarn is "pushed" from the back to the front, using a special tool.

Like any good fiber "addict," I've tried them all, and found Nantucket style suits me the best. I prefer the feel of yarn in my hands, as I work it with the hook, it is very malleable, it fills in the space and goes where you want it. I also really like working from the front, so I can always see how I'm doing. With punch hooking, you are working from the back.

Sybil, 12"x18", designed and hooked by Linda Rehlinger, wool yarn and wool strips on linen

1930's era rug, 24"x36" wool yarn. Courtesy of Kerry MacPhail

(below left) Hooking "Nantucket" style: In this photo, the backing is wrapped around the legs, creating a "frame" in the lap

(below right) 1920's picture of punch hooking. Courtesy of the Hooked Rug Museum

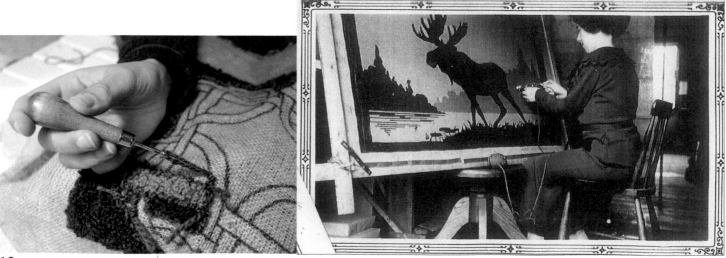

20th Century rug in southwest design, 34"x55" wool yarn on cotton

I encourage you to try them all too, because who knows which will appeal to you? In my case, while I love wool fabric, lets face it, I grow yarn. My 27 sheep and goats lovingly produce piles of wool and mohair, which I spin and send the rest off to be commercially spun for knitting and rug hooking. At this point, I will never run out of yarn. Welcome to my world-- Yarn "R" Us.

Perhaps your world is bursting at the seams with wool fabric. Well, you are in luck. There are hundreds of books on hooking with fabric strips. There are two magazines devoted to hooking with fabric strips (*Rug Hooking Magazine* and *ATHA*), there are dozens of rug retreats happening all over the country, and instruction available in every state of the union. If you search *Amazon.com* for rug hooking books, you will find upwards of 300 books to choose from. All of these will satisfy your curiosity about fabric strips, but none will tell you how to hook with yarn in the Nantucket style!

Judy, hand-shearing one of her Jacob Sheep

Edeldal Farm

Jacob Farm Rug, designed by Judy Taylor, hooked by Michele LeBlanc 36"x25" handspun yarn on linen.

The only exception is my first book, *Hooking With Yarn* (now out of print). At the time of its release, there were no other books on hooking in the Nantucket style. Believe it or not, there are still sellers who will part with a used copy for upwards of $1500.00 (the original price was $17.95)! That gives you some indication of the interest in yarn-hooking that has yet to be fulfilled!

When I decided to write this book, I thought I might feature the work of the other fine yarn-hookers that I have met over the years. I didn't advertise, I just e-mailed a few folks and hoped I'd get a few rugs to share in the book. I got over 100 submissions. I had to stop accepting rugs for lack of space! That is another indication of the enthusiasm for yarn-hooking.

Now, what about punch hooking? Well, there are some great books on the subject, and shops that offer kits and supplies. Interestingly, a few of the rugs in this book were "punched" but I defy you to tell me which!

Burzies Cottage, designed and hooked by Dianne Cross 18"x15" wool yarn on linen

14

Lady Peckett , designed by Rittermere Hurst Field.  Hooked by Gail Sherman Feetham,  24"x36" wool yarn on linen

The difference in the styles is in the hooking, not the end result (pushing vs. pulling the loops).

All of these styles share the same attraction-- they allow for unlimited creativity making durable, long-lasting rugs.

Summer Sunflowers, designed and hooked by Linda Rehlinger, 34"x48" handspun yarn and wool strips on burlap

Rose Rug, 31" round, designed and hooked by Judy Taylor, handspun and commercial yarn on linen

Rug hooking has long been the go-to craft when re-using or recycling yarns from other projects. The yarn in this sweater (left) was ingeniously re-used in the Failte rug ( below).

"Failte" (Welcome), designed and hooked by Dianne Warren. 30"x50" wool yarn (from sweater) on linen

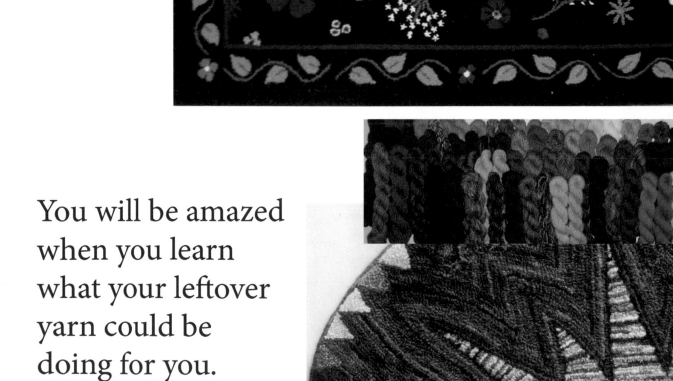

You will be amazed when you learn what your leftover yarn could be doing for you. More on recycling in Chapter 9!

# Chapter 2

# Sundries you'll
# need to hook
# with yarn

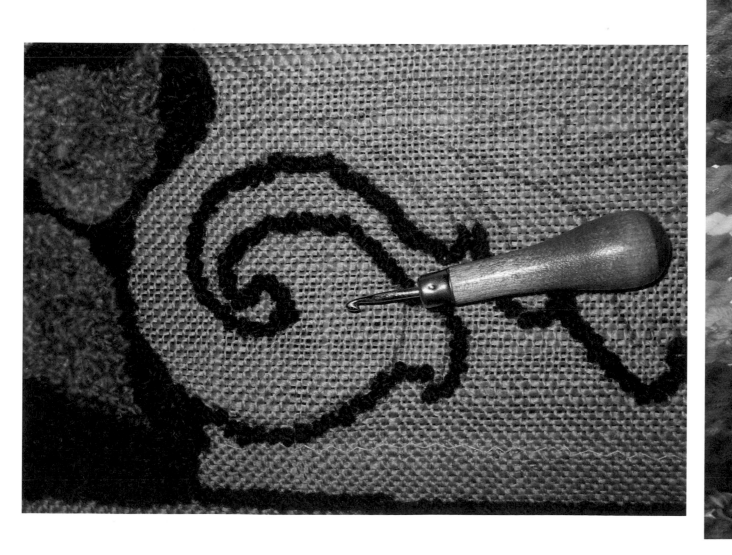

Midnight Garden, designed and hooked by Gail Sherman Feetham.  14"x18" wool yarn on wool fabric, hooked with a fine hook

Pair of Cheticamp coasters, 3" round, courtesy of Michele LeBlanc

Like the pioneers of old, you don't need a lot of fancy stuff to get started. The hook is the main thing, and you really only need one. Unlike knitting needles or crochet hooks, you don't need different sizes to hook different types of projects. Since you only need one hook, you can splurge and treat yourself to fancy wood or ergonomic handles, but I just use the plain-old "workhorse" from Cushing & Co. I prefer a "special O" sized hook, because it works best with linen or burlap backing. If you like hooking on a tighter weave fabric, you might want a finer hook, but the "special O" works great for me, and besides, it makes me feel special.

There are three main backing fabrics used in rug hooking: burlap, linen and monk's cloth. Burlap is inexpensive and available in any fabric store, but it doesn't wash well, so it's not ideal for floor rugs. Linen is washable, and is by far the most durable backing fabric--perfect for rugs that you want to last for hundreds of years. It is more expensive than burlap, but remember: the main expense of creating a hooked rug is in *the time it takes to make it*, not the cost of materials. You will spend exactly as much time hooking a rug on burlap as you will on linen, but the linen rug will last ten times longer!

The third material is Monk's cloth. Monk's cloth is cotton, and can be purchased from some fabric stores and rug hooking companies. Cotton is washable, but not quite as durable as linen. It is the preferred backing for punch hooking because the punch hook goes smoothly through.

When hooking Nantucket-style, you can wrap the backing around your legs, so your lap becomes your "frame." This is how I start out my beginner students. If they find they love hooking with yarn, they can "graduate" to hooking with a frame. I have tried all the frames on the market, and ended up designing a simple frame that works great for me (it also works for quilting and embroidery). You can purchase this frame ready-made, but later in the book you will find the instructions for making one for yourself. If you are at all handy with a saw and glue, you can make a strong, lightweight frame customized just for yourself.

Hooking with the backing fabric around the legs. Your lap becomes your "frame".

Hooking on a lap frame, designed especially for rug hookiing

A few of the great yarns I use for rug hooking. Pictured: handspun, Ewenique, Patons Bulky, Reynold's Lopi, Rowan Big Wool, Halcyon Deco and Rug Wool, Briggs & Little Super, Peace Fleece, Cascade Yarns, Universal Deluxe Chunky, Araucania, Sensations Licorice, New Zealand Woolpack.

Which yarns work best for rug hooking? Oh my gosh, there are so many! You certainly don't need your own flock of sheep to find great yarns for rug hooking. A good rug hooking yarn is a worsted weight to bulky yarn. If you look at the knitting gauge on the label, a yarn that will knit 3.5-4 stitches per inch will work great for rug hooking. We usually use 100% wool yarn, although many blends will work too. The main thing is that the yarn should not be slippery. We are looking for yarns with some texture to them.

Some of the many brands you can choose from include Halcyon Rug Wool and Halcyon Deco, Peace Fleece, Briggs & Little Super Bulky and Atlantic 3-ply, Ewenique Yarn, and many, many others. Single-ply yarns like Lamb's Pride hook up great but are not as durable as a plied yarn.

If you are a hand spinner, look for the "long wools" like Romney, Lincoln, Border Leicester, Navajo and Coopworth. These make fantastic fibers for rug making.

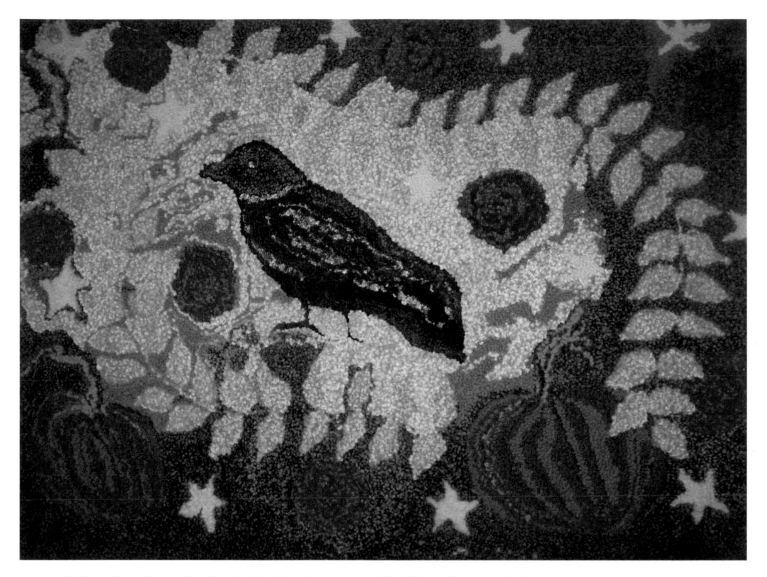

Crow with Pumpkins, designed and hooked by Maya Drummond, 46"x64" mixed yarns on burlap

(right) Hooked farm sign, adapted and hooked by Susie Wilson, 44"x45" handspun Border Leicester wool on linen.

(below) Taylor at her spinning wheel

Box O' Crayons, 24.5x69.5" designed and hooked by Judy Taylor, wool yarn on linen

Remember the yarn array on page 8? All of the yarn in this Box 'O Crayons rug came from the yarn in that shot!

Stars Rug, 29.5"x20" designed and hooked by Judy Taylor, wool yarn on linen

# Chapter 3

# Learning to hook

Photo by Cherie Langlois

Figure 1

Figure 2

Figure 3 (view from underneath)

Figure 4 (view from underneath)

Figure 5 (view from underneath)

Figure 6 (view from underneath)

In this chapter you'll find the basic instructions for hooking with yarn. Each project in this book illustrates the basic techniques in greater detail, so you can build on your skills with each one.

To begin hooking with yarn: Sit with your knees comfortably apart (about 9") with the backing across your lap (design side up). Tuck the backing snugly under the outside of your thighs, so that you can pull the backing somewhat taut across your lap: your lap becomes your "frame" (you can also use frames that are specially designed for Nantucket rug hooking, more about that later).

Hold the hook in your right hand (if you are right-handed) and have the ball of yarn that you are working with between your legs under the backing. Hold the yarn with your left hand under the backing. Your left hand should go underneath on the inside of the backing, rather than trying to reach around the outside to hold your yarn. If you are starting with a small kit, you might be able to get away with reaching around the outside (although to me it seems uncomfortable); but when you get to hooking larger projects like floor rugs, you won't be able to reach around at all. Think of it like you're holding a plate in front of you, with one hand above and one hand underneath.

Push in the hook where you want to begin. For your very first try at rug hooking, I recommend starting with a solid-colored area so you can get the "hang" of it before you attempt to do the detail areas. Later, when you understand the hooking process better, you will always want to begin with the detailed sections, because the pattern lines tend to get obscured when you hook around them. But for your first time hooking, just start in the background area until you get an idea of how far apart to place your loops. (Figure 1)

Push your hook through the backing, from the top, and connect with the yarn below; then pull the end up through the backing, to the top. Leave about a 1" 'tail' of yarn sticking up for now. You will cut this off later, but you need to leave it in place for the time being. Next choose a hole near the tail (usually right next to the tail, or skipping one thread in the backing, depending on how thick the yarn is) and put your hook in again, down through the backing. (Figure 2)

Your left hand can hold up the backing initially, so you have something to push your hook against (Figure 3), until you get your hook through, but then "slide" down the yarn with your left hand for a couple of inches. Notice that I am not letting the yarn flop around underneath, I have it under control in my left hand all the time. (Figure 4)

Then, still holding the yarn underneath with your left hand, lift that part of the yarn up, push the hook down from the top, and connect the yarn between your left thumb and fingers onto your hook.

It really helps if you hold the yarn on the hook with your left hand until you pull the loop through to the top. This keeps the yarn connected to the hook, so you avoid "splitting the yarn." (Figure 5)

Once you have pulled the yarn through to the top, let go with your left hand underneath and feel the slack in the yarn pulling up. (Figures 6 and 7 show the slack pulling up after the hook has been pulled through to the top.)

As soon as you feel with your left hand that you have pulled up all the yarn, stop pulling from above. The reason to give yourself that slack in the yarn is so that you do not pull out the previous loop. (Figure 8 shows the slack pulled snug in the back. Figure 9 shows what the right hand is doing at the same time)

Figure 7 (view from underneath)

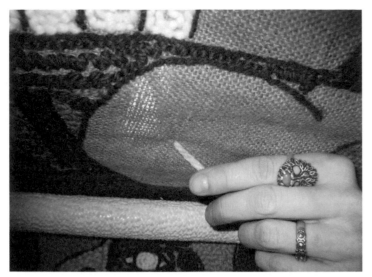

Figure 8 (view from underneath)

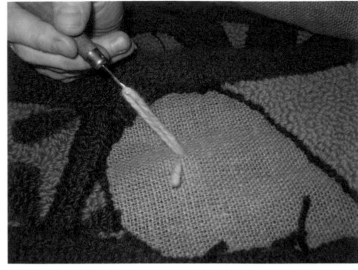

Figure 9

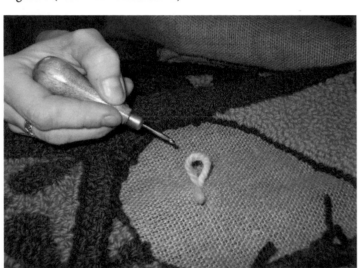

Figure 10

Figure 11

Figure 12

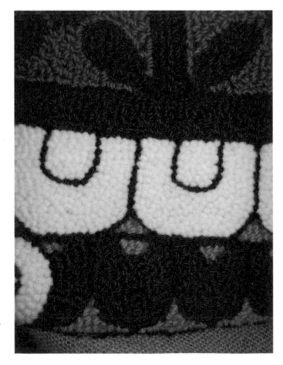

Figure 13

Figure 14. Closeup of Card Trick, floor rug designed and hooked by Teresa Waldo, finished rug measures 31"x21" wool yarn on linen. Notice the short, densely packed loops.

Figure 15. Spirit Dance, wall hanging designed by Patti Armstrong, hooked by Andrea Hammel, 20"x24" wool yarn on burlap. Notice the sculpted effect in her design.

Next, with your left hand, pull the loop on top of the backing (Figure 10) down to the desired height, usually about 1/8 of an inch. In general, the loop should be about as tall as the yarn is wide (Figure 11). If you are making a floor rug--where durability is the goal--short, densely packed loops wear the best (Figure 14). However, if you are making a wall-hanging, you can make your loops a little higher (Figure 15). Practice making all your loops the same height. Notice that if you do not give yourself enough slack in the yarn, you are liable to pull out the previous loop.

When you come to the end of a section and you want to switch to a different yarn or a different area of the rug, bring up the last loop, just as if you were going to make another loop, but this time cut the yarn on the top and pull the remaining yarn out the back with your left hand. Now you have two tails sticking up, one when you began and one when you finished. These tails need to remain in place until they are surrounded by other loops, at which time you can cut them from

above, even with the loops around them. They are held in place by the pressure of the loops around them, and they seem to disappear. (In Figure 12, the tails are sticking up and surrounded, Figure 13 shows the trimmed tails which seem to disappear.)

It may seem precarious to leave the tails like that without tying a knot or anything, but in fact, this is one of the keys to the longevity of these hooked rugs. Sometime during the life of this rug, ten, twenty, fifty years from now, that rug may need to be repaired. Because we do not tie knots, we can always pull out yarn in the damaged areas and re-hook them. The loops in hooked rugs should not pull out with normal wear and tear (walking on them, vacuuming or washing), but occasionally a bit of yarn can get snagged (kitties are often the culprit!), stained or worn, and what is so great about these rugs is that they can always be repaired. (Figures 16-19 show typical damage, and the same areas after rehooking)

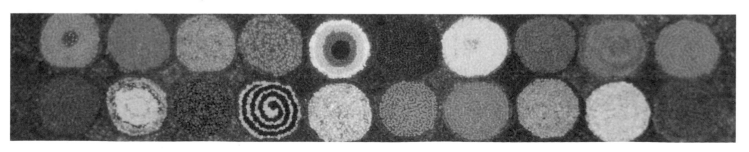

Figure 16. Yikes! Kitty play with rug! Bad Kitty!

Figure 17. Oh well, no harm done.

Figure 18. This time the perp was a doggie.

Figure 19. Good as new

More on how far apart to place your loops: The goal with Nantucket rug hooking is that you want your loops close enough together so that you cannot see the backing from the front, but not so close that the rug won't lie flat. You need to hook for a little while to really get this concept, but remember that the loops need room to spread out (this is what keeps them in place, they spread out above the backing).

If you are over hooking, you will notice that, after you've hooked a section, the edges tend to curl when you let go of the rug. A little curling is okay while the yarn "settles," but too much over packing will prevent your rug from lying flat when you lay it on the floor or hang it on the wall. If a section is badly over packed, it's best to pull out the yarn and start again. (Figures 20 and 21)

You also want to avoid underpacking your loops. Figure 22 shows a small gap in the hooking of the scallop, Figure 23 shows what it looks like when a few more loops are brought in.

One of the wonderful things about hooking with yarn is that it is squishy. Once a loop is surrounded, it just "wants" to be where you want it to be. It is malleable, it can be adjusted by the placement of the loops around it. Notice how the outline in Figure 24 appears uneven and jagged. Hooking an oval line on a woven grid can be problematic, but when the surrounding colors are brought in, the line appears smooth and curved as intended. (Figure 24 shows the rows seeming uneven, Figure 25 shows the lines appear smooth and unbroken because of the hooking around them.)

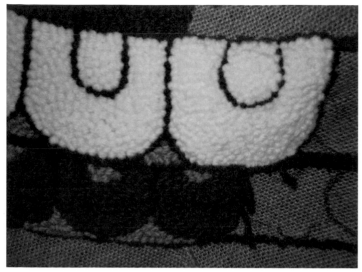

Figure 20. The scallop on the right is over packed. Notice how it curls at the edges.

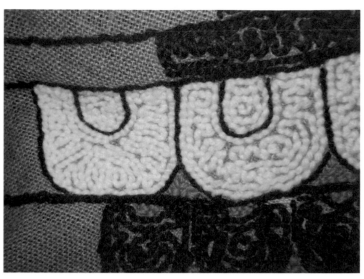

Figure 21. Underside view: the over packed scallop is on the left. Notice how there are fewer gaps between the rows of hooking where there is over-packing.

Figure 22. Underpacking. Notice the gap on the lower right corner of the scallop

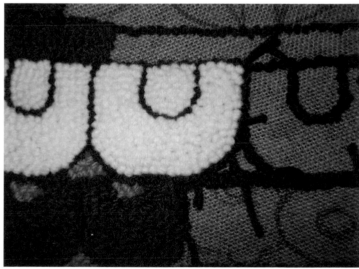

Figure 23. Same area, after bringing up a tail, hooking a few loops, and then the ending tail. The tails are surrounded, so they can be cut off.

Figure 24. This row seems uneven.

Figure 25. Same row looks smoother after it is surrounded

Special instructions for hooking with fabric strips:

Both yarn and fabric strips are traditional, and can certainly be used together in the same project, but the technique for hooking with fabric strips is slightly different. For one thing, fabric strips look very rectangular, so they give a different textural look to the rug. I tend to prefer hooking in straight lines when using the fabric strips, because they fit so nicely together (as opposed to the yarn loops, that are round and just fill in the space all around them). However, you can also hook in rounded patterns, as long as you are careful about the back of the strip (on the back of the rug). You want to be careful that your strip does not get twisted across the back (this would leave a bump that might catch on something later). So for best results, when you push in your hook to grab the strip from below, pick up the strip close to the last loop, and carefully lift it up through the backing.

When we hook with yarn, we can give ourselves lots of "slack" in the yarn, pulling up until the yarn pulls tight against the back; then we pull the remaining yarn down. But this is not the recommended way to hook with fabric strips. It is too easy to twist the strip if you give yourself a lot of slack to pull up on. Also, the process is too rough on the cut edges of the strip, and your rug will end up looking more like a terrycloth towel! Figure 26 shows the strip end pulled to the top, and the hook is ready to make the first loop. Figure 27 shows how closely the hook connects with the strip to avoid roughing the edges of the strip.

As for your beginning and ending tails, they are cut off even with the surrounding loops, just as you do with yarn. More complete instruction on hooking with fabric strips can be found at your local library and the internet. Instructional texts on hooking with fabric strips are numerous and varied.

Why the difference in technique when hooking with yarn or fabric strips? You could hook with yarn using the same careful technique that we use with fabric strips, but you would be giving up one of yarn's greatest advantages to your hooking: speed. The method of hooking with yarn involves more steps at first, and you may feel "all thumbs" getting the hang of getting the yarn on the hook, and making the loops; but the fact is that the steps make the process more automatic, because you only have to do one thing at a time. When

30

hooking with fabric strips, you must get your fabric on the hook, avoid twisting the strip and prevent roughing up the edges, all with one complicated movement, so it tends to be a slower and more careful process.

If you've ever learned to knit or crochet with yarn, you know that it seems complicated at first; you feel like you have to think about each step. But by and by, you find you're knitting automatically, without looking at the yarn and needles, having a conversation, watching TV, and so on. That's exactly how it is hooking with yarn. You just get used to the feel of each step, and before you know it, you're doing it by instinct.

For me, it's the process of hooking that I enjoy the most. I don't really care how long it takes me to hook a rug, because I so thoroughly enjoy hooking: the process itself is soothing and tactilely satisfying, and progress is constant and steady. So I wouldn't emphasize the greater speed of hooking with yarn, but let's face it, we all like to see some progress, and I do enjoy being able to get more done. How you hook is less important than how you enjoy the experience. So whether you like to punch your loops or pull them, whether you prefer yarn or fabric strips, ultimately all of these methods give you the freedom and creativity to make beautiful rugs, you just need to find the one that suits you the best.

Figure 26, hooking with fabric strips

Figure 27, view from underneath

Figure 28. Only a small amount of fabric strip will be pulled up. View from below

Figure 29. View from above: gently pull the strip up until it pulls tight across the back.

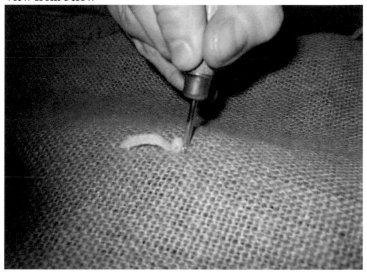

Figure 30. The hook is ready to make the second loop.

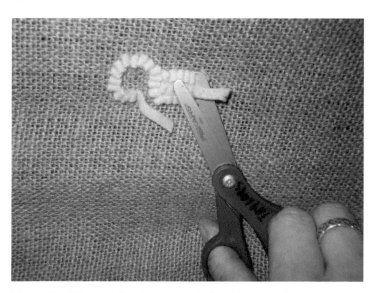

Figure 31. The end that is surrounded can be cut off.

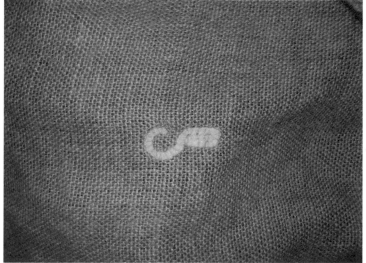

Figure 32. View from the underside. Notice that there is very little space between the rows. Fabric strips don't spread out on top like yarn.

Finishing and Hemming

The way that you finish your rug depends on how you plan to use it. For a wall hanging, a simple turned under hem can be sufficient. Once you have hooked your second project, "Dutch Treat" (Chapter 6), cut the backing 2 to 3 inches from the hooked edge (Figure 33). Since this project has a rounded edge, turn under and baste with a needle and thread along the foldline. Pull the basting thread so the burlap will lie flat along the fold line. Pin in place. (Figure 34) It is important to dig deep with your stitches. Make sure you are grabbing the backing with your needle, not a bit of yarn.

If you are hemming corners on a rectangular rug, like the "Celtic Mat" project in Chapter 7, first cut away the corner edge of the backing, so it will not add extra bulk to the corner hem (Figure 35). Then you can fold the extra backing underneath to make a mitred corner which should lie nice and flat (Figure 36).

If you are designing a rug for the floor, like the "Waste Not, Want Not" rug project in Chapter 8, it is important to bind the edges of the rug before you hem. For this process, purchase cotton cording from the fabric store (3/16" works well). Wrap your backing around the cord, so the backing extends beyond the hooked edge and with a needle and thread, and then tack the cording in place all around the outside of the rug. (Figure 37) You will find more detailed instructions for this technique in Chapter 8.

Pin the extra backing under, but don't hem it yet. With matching yarn on a darning needle, push the needle in at the base of the cording (close to the hooked edge) on the back side of the rug. Pull the yarn through so that there is a 1" tail sticking out the back. Fold the tail under and whip stitch around the cording a few times (sewing over the tail). Then you will want to turn the stitches around so that your end tail comes out the back when you finish that length of yarn. Put your needle in at the base of the cording from the front this time, and pull the yarn through to the back. Then continue to whip stitch all around the outside of the rug. When you run out of yarn, start a new length of yarn in the same way (going in from the back for the first few stitches, then turning the stitching around so you are coming in from the front) and this time you will be whip stitching over two tails. When you come to the

32

very end, put your needle through the whip stitching in the back, and come out about one inch from your last stitch. You can cut the end off close to where it came out. A more detailed illustration of this technique is covered in project #4, (Chapter 8).

Next, hem your rug in the same way as you would a wall hanging, making sure that you dig deep with your stitches so they will hold (you may have to move your pins after you have bound the edge). The goal is not to make dainty, invisible stitches. If you ever have to repair this rug (or if your granddaughter has to repair it!), you will appreciate it if the stitches are easy to find, and you don't have to go digging around looking for them. (This process is covered in detail in Chapter 8)

Figure 33

Figure 34

Figure 35

Figure 36

Figure 37. This process is covered step by step in Chapter 9.

No Latex Backing!

If you mastered the hooking technique, your rug will not fall apart with normal wear and tear. No glue or latex is necessary to hold the rug together; in fact, latex can be very damaging to a rug. Contrary to what you might think, latex does not prevent the loops from being pulled out. If they are snagged, they'll pull out, but they will be impossible to re-hook! Not only that, but if you wash a rug with latex on the back, you will very likely cause the rug to rot because of poor air circulation. Just remember, this craft was invented hundreds of years ago, long before the invention of latex, and those rugs held up very nicely, thank you very much. If you want to prevent a rug slipping on a hardwood floor, you can purchase a rubber mat at a carpet store, and cut it so it is the same shape as your rug.

Worn edge on a rug from the 1940's. If this edge had been bound, this damage could have been prevented.

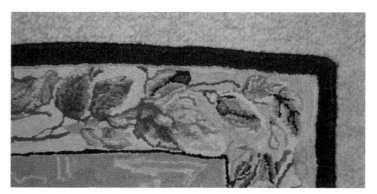

The damaged area has been patched and rehooked, and the edge bound, so now the rug can be enjoyed for many years to come.

Washing a rug

## Care and Cleaning

Vacuuming is very good for hooked rugs, since it removes the grit that tends to wear away the fiber. However, I always examine the rug, top and bottom, prior to vacuuming, to make sure no yarn has been pulled out. If you do find a loose piece, just re-hook it before you vacuum.

To wash your hooked rug, dissolve about one tablespoon of laundry detergent (you want laundry detergent as opposed to dish-washing liquid because it won't make suds) in about 2 cups of cold water (I'm told that a dash of vinegar is also good for the wool). Put in a clean rag and squeeze it almost all the way out. You don't need to get the rug soaking wet, you just want to use enough moisture to lift the grit and hair off the surface of the rug. After you have scrubbed a small section, rinse the rag in clean water and go over that

Lady Teasle likes to "supervise" the work, from my lap.

section again, so you rinse out some of the soap. Continue the process on the top and bottom of the rug. Then lay it somewhere where it can get plenty of air circulation while it dries. Don't 'beat' a hooked rug, as this is too hard on the backing material.

In Days of Yore, our ancestors would wait for a good powdery snow, take their rugs outside, throw snow on the top, sweep it off, and bring the rugs inside to dry! So you just need enough moisture to lift the grit off the surface.

## Designing Your Own Rugs

Burlap is a great backing material to use as long as you don't intend to wash the item regularly. Burlap rots when it gets wet. We live in the Green River Valley in western Washington State, and we are often flooded in the winter. Last year, we thought we were so clever, because we piled all of our sandbags in the spring and covered them with tarps to keep them dry all summer to avoid having to fill and haul new bags next year. Don't you know, when we unveiled them the next fall, we had a big pile of sand with shreds of burlap throughout! So burlap is fine for pillows and stuffed animals, small wall-hangings etc., but linen is best for floor rugs (too bad they don't make sandbags out of linen!).

Linen is made from flax. When the flax plant is prepared to be spun into linen, the plant is soaked in water, and everything that doesn't rot is what is spun into linen. Linen backing guarantees that your floor rug will last as long as possible. Linen is quite a bit more expensive than burlap, but don't be tempted to go with the cheaper option. By far, the greatest value that you will put in your hooked rug is your time and labor. You will spend just as much on the yarn, and you will spend just as long hooking the rug, but the final project will survive only a fraction of the time as a rug with a linen foundation.

I start my design on a piece of paper that is the size of the finished project. With a pencil at first, I experiment with the design elements, erasing and moving things as necessary until I'm satisfied with the design. Then I go over all the pencil lines with a Sharpie Pen. Next I lay window screen (available by the roll at a hardware store) over the paper design, and again trace over all of the lines with a Sharpie. Now I have an exact representation of the drawing I did on paper.

I lay the window screen on my linen backing and go over the lines again, this time transferring them to the linen. I like to go over the lines one more time on the linen after I have removed the window screen so they show up better. (Figure 38)

Figure 38. Getting your design on the backing. This process is covered in detail in Chapter 5.

Don't worry about drawing with a permanent marker if you don't know exactly what you want. You can always change your mind later. What you draw on the backing is not going to show on the finished product. Sometimes you just have to hook an area before you can tell if the drawing is going to work. You can always change your mind and change the design. You need a permanent marker though so the ink won't bleed into your rug when you wash it, or rub off while you are hooking.

When color-planning your rug, go back to the paper design you started with, and grab those crayons.

Experiment with different color combinations until you are satisfied. The nice thing about coloring with crayons is that the mark you make is about the same width as a loop of yarn, so you can decide how to do your detailed areas ahead of time, as you color it with crayons in about the same proportions as you'll use with the yarn, in hooking the rug.

I recommend having about 4 oz. of yarn per square foot of hooked area. Now, unless you are Super Math Man, you will have to do a bit of guesswork, to determine the square footage of a particular color in your design. If you are going to be working with a yarn that you have aplenty, then 4 oz per square foot is a good

foot of hooked area. Now, unless you are Super Math Man, you will have to do a bit of guesswork, to determine the square footage of a particular color in your design. If you are going to be working with a yarn that you have aplenty, then 4 oz per square foot is a good guide. However, if you are working with something special that is limited in quantity (like a hand-dyed, variegated yarn), you might want to have 6 oz on hand for each square foot.

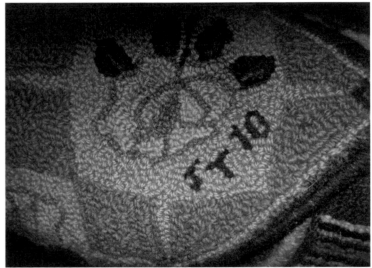

Figure 39

guide. However, if you are working with something special that is limited in quantity (like a hand-dyed, variegated yarn), you might want to have 6 oz on hand for each square foot.

I always recommend incorporating your initials and the year somewhere in the hooked area of the rug. You can also sign your rug on the back, or include a label, but the only authentic way to date your rugs (therefore to value them) is to hook your name and date right into the design. (Figure 39) I have many treasured antique rugs, but unfortunately, it is rare to find an old rug that has been signed and dated.

Lady Teasle puts in another hour of hard work on the rug.

This unfinished rug probably dates from the 1960's, and was hooked with fabric strips. I finished it with yarn. Believe it or not, I didn't even have to dye any yarn for this project. Either I found the colors in my "stash" or I was able to buy commercial yarn in the colors I needed. If you put your nose right up to the rug, you can tell which side was hooked with fabric or which with yarn, but from a distance, it appears seamless. If I wanted to finish this project with fabric strips, I would surely have had to go to the dye pot, and the color changes would have been more obvious. Lucky for me, we live in a world where beautiful yarns are available in practically any color we like!

(above) Unfinished antique hooked rug, designer unknown

(left) Same rug, finished by Judy Taylor, 36.5"x24.5" wool strips and wool yarn on burlap.

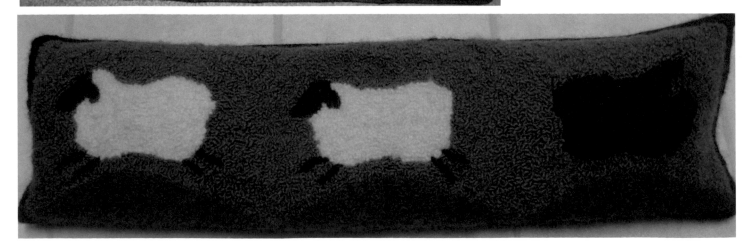

Black Sheep of the Family, designed by Angela Jones, hooked by Kerry MacPhail, 7"x28" wool yarn on monk's cloth

Chinese Basket, 12"x14"  designer unknown, hooked by Judy Taylor, commercial and handspun wool yarn on burlap

Caucas, designed and hooked by Rosemary Thomas 42"x64" wool yarn on rug warp

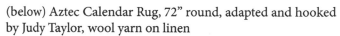

(below) Aztec Calendar Rug, 72" round, adapted and hooked by Judy Taylor, wool yarn on linen

Nick's Dream, adapted from a design by Helina Tilk, hooked by Nancy Forsman, 31"x21.5" handspun yarn on linen

Tess Rug, designed and hooked by Judy Taylor,
17.5"x30.5" handspun yarn on linen

Stars and Hearts, designed and hooked by Maya Drummond,
22"x24" wool and acrylic yarns on monks cloth

# Chapter 4  Gallery

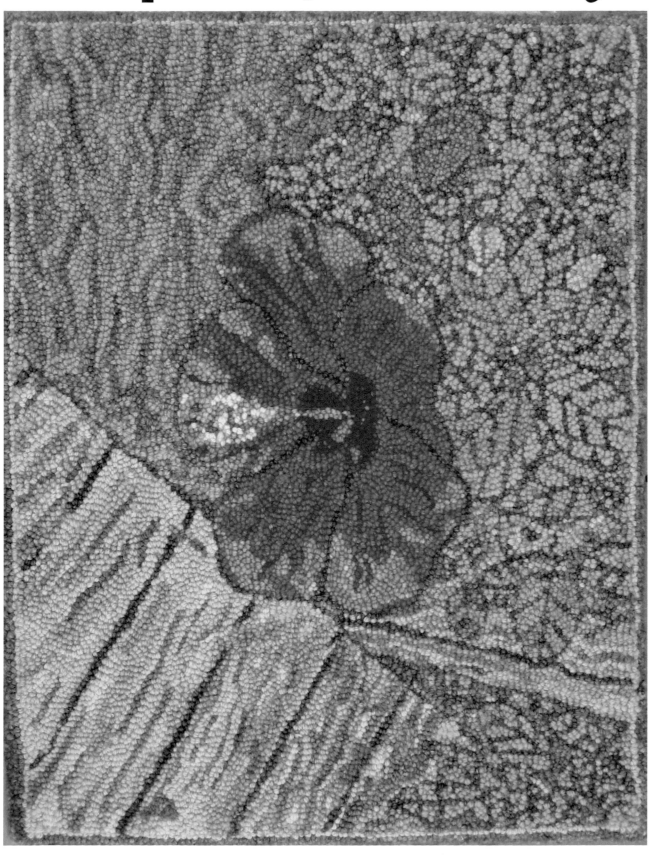

Rockport Hibiscus, Designed and hooked by Steve Grappe,
29"x23" wool yarn on monk's cloth

The Great Barrier Reef, designed and hooked by
Bonnie Campbell, 37"x20.5" wool yarn on linen

Hook Line & Sinker, designed and hooked by Jill Purcell, 20"x12.5" wool yarn
and nylons on linen

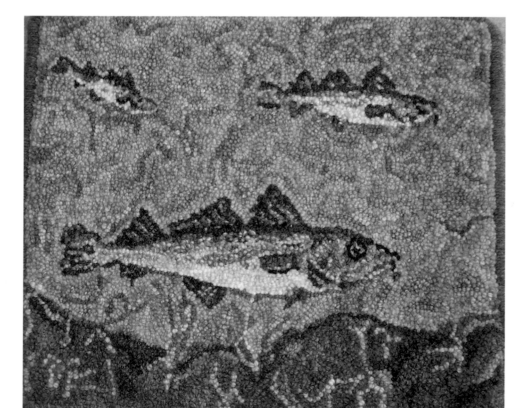

Cod, designed and hooked by Venissa Fancy, 13"x15" wool yarn on burlap

Stained Glass Rug, designed and hooked by Judy Taylor, 27" round, Ewenique yarn on linen

Violin, designed and hooked by Maya Drummond, 22"x48" mixed yarn and fabric strips on linen

Rooster Rug, designed and hooked by Judy Taylor, 18"x26" wool yarn on linen

Rooster Rug, designed by Judy Taylor, Hooked by Doreen Garrod, 18"x26" wool yarn on linen

Bayeux Tapestry, Adapted and hooked by Judy Taylor, 66"x20" wool yarn on linen

A Grub Box, designed
and hooked by Venissa
Fancy, 21"x15" wool yarn
on burlap

Divied Light, designed and hooked by Steve Grappe, 20"x26" wool yarn on monk's cloth

Spectacular, designed by Violet Young, hooked by Lyle Gowing, 32"x42" wool
yarn on burlap.

A Self Portrait, designed and hooked by Bonnie Campbell, 36"x41" wool yarn and roving on linen.

Betty's Cat, designed by Amanda Ladd, hooked by Pam Langdon 24"x36" wool yarn and wool strips on monk's cloth

Penny, Pasha and Jezebel, designed and hooked by Judy Taylor, 21"x32.5" hand-spun yarn on linen.

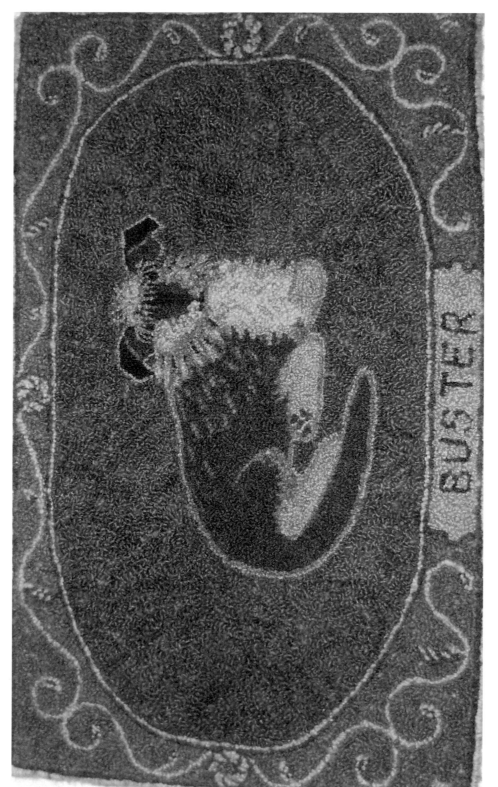

Buster Rug, designed and hooked by Judy Taylor, 17.5"x30.5"  handspun yarn on linen

Outhouse, designed and hooked by Dianne Warren, 13"x16" wool yarn on linen

Fall Leaves, designed and hooked by Gail Sherman Feetham, 30"x38" wool yarn on burlap

Meditation Rug, designed and hooked by Jill Purcell, 40"x27" handspun and commercial yarn on linen

Sunflowers, 25"x35" designed and hooked by Betty Pennell, wool yarn on burlap

Stars and Hearts pillow, designed and hooked by Patti Finch, 14"x14" wool yarn on burlap

Sunflowers, designed and hooked by Venissa Fancy, 22"x19" wool yarn on burlap

Cook's Harbour Scroll, adapted by Ruth Chaffey, hooked by Dianne Warren, 25"x37" wool yarn on burlap

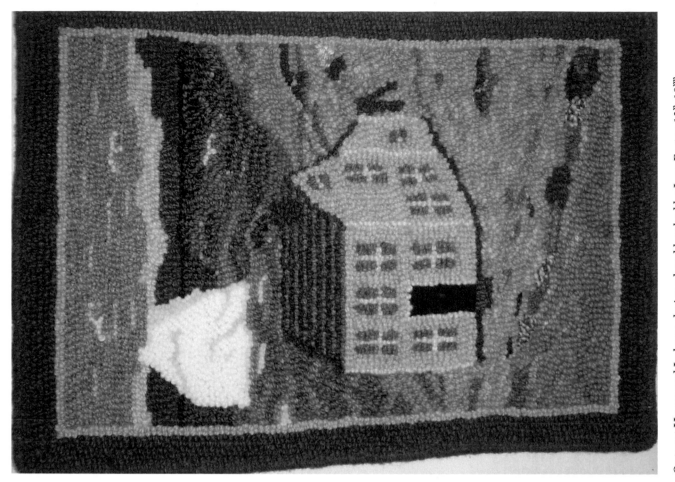

Outport House and Iceberg, designed and hooked by Joan Foster, 13"x18""" handspun yarn on linen

Welcome Rug, designed and hooked by Jill Purcell, 12"x18" handspun yarn on linen

54

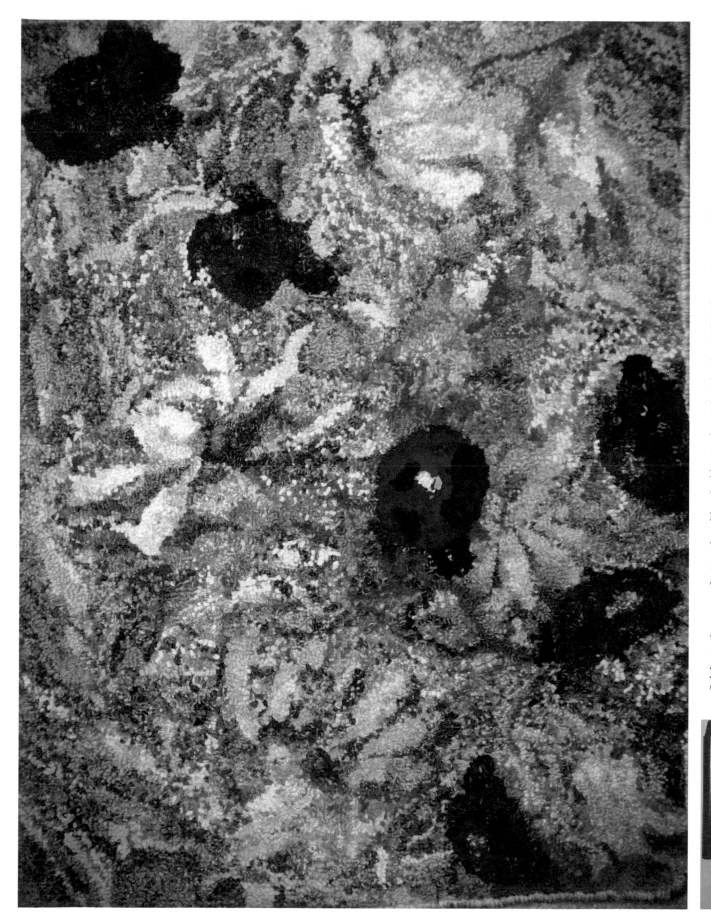

Celebrate Summer, designed and hooked by Andrea Rheinlander, 28"x18" wool yarn on linen

Family Crest Rug, designed and hooked by Cole Adams, 54"x34" wool yarn on linen.

A Day at Corner Brook, designed and hooked by Tina Stewart, 20"x30" wool and synthetic yarn on burlap

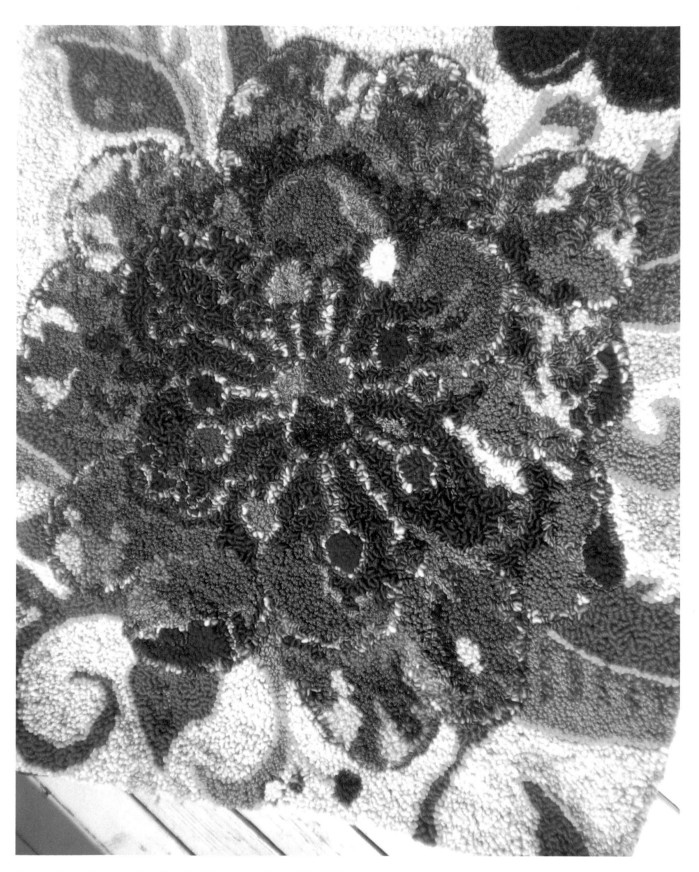

Power Peony, Designed and hooked by Cole Adams, 54"x34" wool yarn on linen

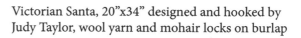

Victorian Santa, 20"x34" designed and hooked by
Judy Taylor, wool yarn and mohair locks on burlap

St. Nick in Forest, designed and hooked by Judy Taylor, 3'x5'
wool yarn and mohair locks on burlap

Winter Scene" (designer unknown) hooked by Janette
Lambert, 17"x18" wool and synthetic yarn on burlap

Floral, Designed by Caron, hooked by Teresa Waldo, 20"x28" wool yarn on burlap

Fish Pond, designed and hooked by Dianne Warren 10"x16"
wool yarn on burlap

Jumping Whale, adapted and hooked by Judy Taylor, 24"x30" handspun yarn on linen

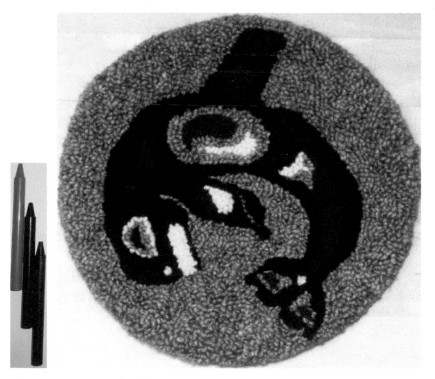

Whale Pillow, adapted and hooked by Judy Taylor, 21" round, commercial yarn on burlap

Haida Single Mortuary Totem Pole, adapted and hooked by Rosemary Thomas, 24"x55" wool yarn on linen

Navajo Impression, designed
and hooked by Jill Purcell,
30"x21" handspun yarn on
linen

Salmon And Roe, adapted and hooked by Stephanie Ellyas,
fish 24"x30" roe 10" round, wool yarn on linen

Double Salmon wall hanging, adapted and
hooked by Stephanie Ellyas, 18"x40" wool yarn
on linen

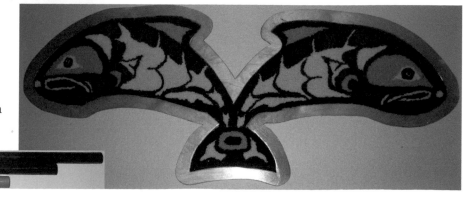

Swans, designed by Bluenose, hooked by Sigrid Grant, 26"x39" wool yarn on burlap

Roses & Diamonds, designed and hooked by Judy Taylor, 26.5"x21" wool yarn on linen

Bear Rug, designed by Nancy Forsman and Laurie Lawson, 30"x36"  handspun yarn on linen

The Birchies, designed and hooked by Dianne Warren, 13"x16" wool yarn and roving on burlap

# Chapter 5
# Project #1
# Teddy Bear

Miss Blue Beary, designed by Judy Taylor, hooked by Ellen Burleson, 10" tall, wool yarn on burlap.

You probably have heard the story of how 'teddy bears' acquired their name--from an incident when Teddy Roosevelt, although an avid hunter, also a renowned good sport, refused to shoot a tied-up bear during a 1902 hunting trip. When the incident became widely known and applauded by most Americans, there was an explosion of notoriety for 'Teddy's bear', and it became both a mascot for his next campaign and a popular stuffed toy for children, in the early 1900's.

Assorted hand-hooked teddy bears, and other stuffed cuties

Diagram of Teddy Bear pieces

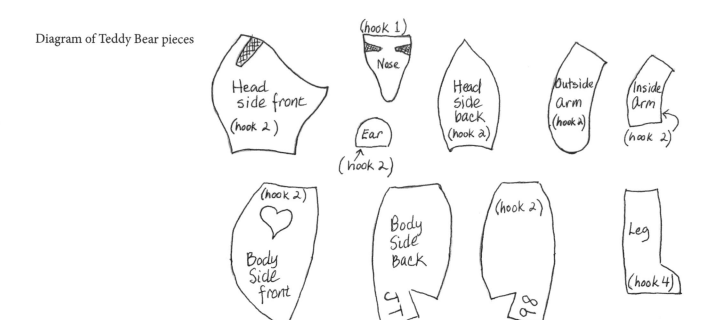

Head side front (hook 2)

Nose (hook 1)

Ear (hook 2)

Head side back (hook 2)

Outside arm (hook 2)

Inside arm (hook 2)

Body Side front (hook 2)

Body Side Back

(hook 2)

Leg (hook 4)

Now's your chance to give rug hooking a try. Stuffed animals make excellent first projects, because you don't have to know how to hook details, you just fill in each pattern piece. This Teddy Bear project is perfect for beginners: all you have to practice is how far apart to place your loops, and learn to get your loops about the same height. For this project you will need:

Rug hook
Scissors
Sharpie Pen
Fiberglass window screen
1 yd. burlap
4 oz main color yarn
2 feet of red or pink for the heart
Felt for eyes and nose
Fabric for paws and ears
Upholstery thread
Regular weight thread
Sewing needle
Polyester stuffing

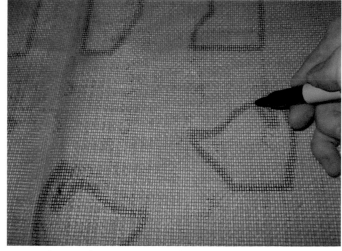

2. Lay the window screen over the burlap, trace over all the lines again

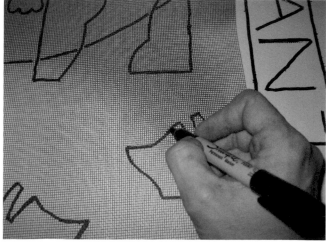

1. Lay window screen over your pattern, trace all the lines with a permanent marker

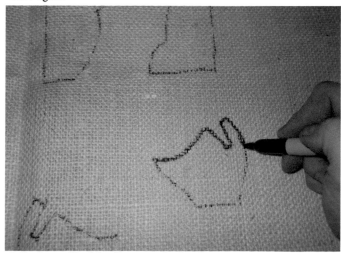

3. Redraw all of the lines on the burlap

You will find a separate area on your paper pattern for your cutout guide for the fabric and felt decorations for your bear. You can pick out a matching fabric for the ears and paws, and felt for the eyes and nose.

If you are using a frame, clamp your burlap, pattern side up, onto the frame. If you're not using a frame, tuck the burlap around the outside of your thighs, so your lap becomes your frame.

It's always best to start in solid-colored areas with your first project, so this one is ideal for perfecting the technique. You can go back to Chapter 3 for a refresher on hooking technique.

## BASIC RUG HOOKING INSTRUCTIONS

Just remember these basic steps for hooking:

1. Push in your hook with your right hand, bring up the tail. (view from above)

2. Push in your hook again, in the next hole.

3. View from below, pushing the hook through the backing

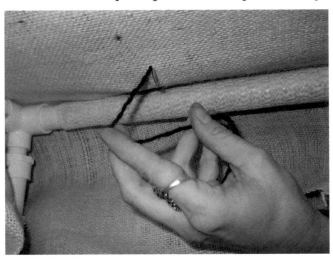

4. With your left hand, slide down the yarn a few inches. Lift that part of the yarn up onto the hook. (View from underneath)

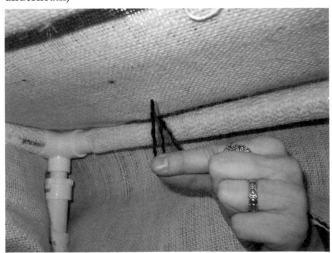

5. Pull down on it to keep it on the hook. (View from underneath)

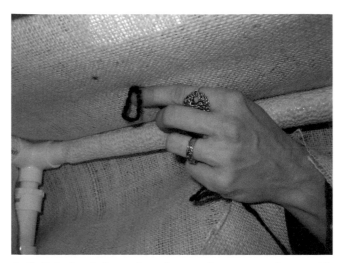

6. Pull the hook through to the top, then you can let go with your left hand; and just feel the slack in the yarn as you pull it up snug against the back. You can feel this with your left hand underneath, but also notice that when you have pulled up all the slack, the tail (or the previous loop) will shift a bit. Careful that you don't pull up too hard, or you might pull out your previous loop.

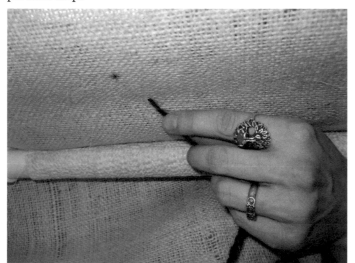

7. Slack pulled tight across the back (view from below)

8. Slack pulled tight across the back (view from above)

9. With your left hand, pull the loop you've just made on the top down to the desired height, usually about 1/8".

10. When you are ready to switch to another color or section, bring up a loop, and before you pull it all the way down, cut it from above so you leave a tail in the front, just like when you began. When those tails are surrounded, they can be cut off, the same height as the surrounding loops. Don't carry the yarn across the back if you are moving to a different area. Just bring up a tail, cut it off, and start with a new tail (or a new color) somewhere else.

I would outline each piece, then fill in, going in whatever direction is comfortable for you. It doesn't matter at all what direction you hook in, as long as one loop is right next to the other.

One tip-- when you start the outline, you should be inside the line one thread or so, then start to hook the outline with your loops. That way your tail will be totally surrounded when you complete the piece. This would also apply to an outside row of a rug project, it's always best to think ahead and make sure all of your tails will be surrounded by loops.

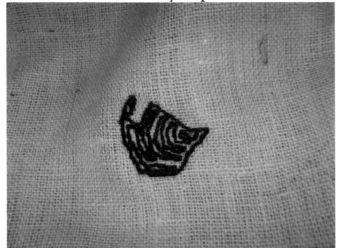

View of the backside of hooked area. Notice the space between the rows where the backing shows through.

Every once in a while, look at the work, both from the top and the underside. On top, you should not be able to see the backing, the yarn should fill in the space as it spreads out on the top. The piece should lie pretty flat when you take it off the frame. On the back, you should be able to see the backing between the rows. If you can't see any backing on the underside, you are probably over packing your loops (see Chapter 3).

The back side of this project is not going to show, since the pieces will be sewn together and stuffed, but getting to know what the back should look like is essential for hooking floor rugs. Notice as you hook the project that your skills will improve, your loops will be more and more even, and spacing will be easier to gauge.

Once you have hooked all the pieces, cut them apart, leaving a generous amount of burlap around each piece. The burlap tends to fray during the sewing process, so you'll want extra. Cut out matching fabric for ears and paws, and felt eyes and nose.

72

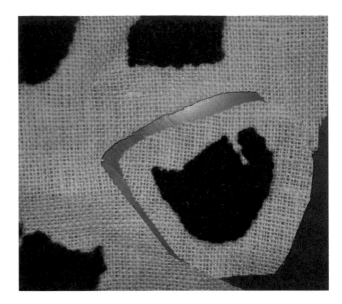

Cut out the hooked pattern pieces, leaving plenty of extra burlap on all sides

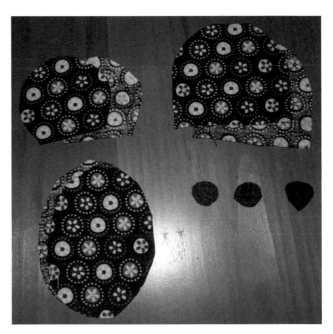

Cut out matching fabric for ears and paws, cut out felt for eyes and nose

## SEWING YOUR BEAR TOGETHER

Step 1: Sew both Head Side Front pieces together as shown, using upholstery thread. Take deep stitches, to create a strong seam. The stitches will be hidden by the hooked loops (outside view)

**Step 1**

**Step 2:** Pin the Nose piece to the Head Side Front pieces, lining up the ear notches (Do not cut the notches). Sew with upholstery thread. (outside view)

**Step 2**

**Step 3:** Trim away the excess, to reduce the bulk. Then tack burlap edge down on inside of Ear. (inside view) Repeat this step for the other Ear.

**Step 3**

**Step 4:** Pin fabric to inside of Ear, and sew with regular weight thread. (This finishes the ear, so all edges are hidden. This view shows the inside of the ear, looking at the fabric side; the hooked side is in back). Repeat this step for the other Ear.

**Step 4**

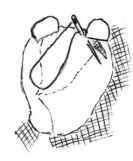

**Step 5:** Sew Ear pieces to Head, in the notched area (the un-hooked area), using upholstery thread. Be sure no burlap shows under the ear pieces. (outside view)

**Step 5**

**Step 6:** Pin felt eyes and nose to Head as shown. Sew with regular weight thread. (outside view)

**Step 6**

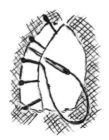

**Step 7:** Sew Head Side Back pieces together as shown, using upholstery thread. (outside view)

**Step 7**

**Step 8:** Sew Head Back to Head Front as shown, with upholstery thread. Stuff head tightly with polyester stuffing. (outside view)

**Step 8**

**Step 9:** Reinforce the hooked edge of the Foot as shown, sewing several stitches with upholstery thread (inside view). Repeat this step for other foot pieces.

**Step 9**

**Step 10:** CAREFULLY cut burlap up to the reinforced edge of Foot piece. Repeat on other leg pieces. (inside view)

**Step 10**

For this photo (right), I had to replace the felt eyes and nose with buttons because the felt just wouldn't show up against the charcoal yarn.

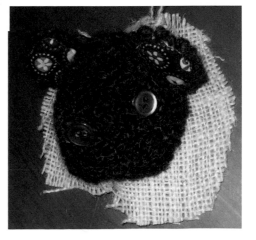

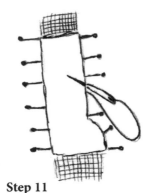

**Step 11**

Step 11: Pin two leg pieces together as shown, sew with upholstery thread. (outside view) Repeat this step for other leg.

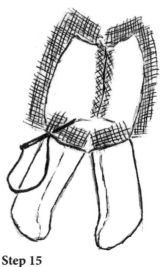

**Step 15**

Step 15: Pin legs to Body Back. Check before sewing that legs are centered, and bear will sit nicely. (You may need to overlap the legs slightly.) Sew with upholstery thread. (This view shows the inside of the Body Back section, and the outside of the legs.)

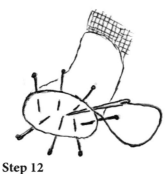

**Step 12**

Step 12: Pin Foot fabric to the bottom of Leg as shown, and repeat this step with the other Leg, adjusting the shape so both feet look the same. Sew the feet with regular thread.
Stuff the legs with polyester stuffing. Stuff foot area tightly, but only lightly stuff the upper legs, so they will allow the bear to sit. (outside view)

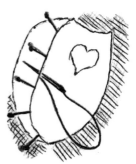

**Step 16**

Step 16: Sew Body Side Front pieces together as shown, using upholstery thread. (outside view)

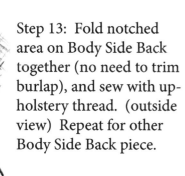

**Step 13**

Step 13: Fold notched area on Body Side Back together (no need to trim burlap), and sew with upholstery thread. (outside view) Repeat for other Body Side Back piece.

**Step 17**

Step 17: Pin Body Front to Body Back, and sew together, using upholstery thread. Check your stitching around legs to conceal burlap. Stuff body tightly with polyester stuffing. (outside view)

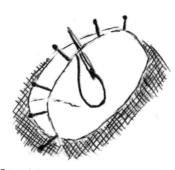

**Step 14**

Step 14: Sew Body Side Back pieces together as shown, using upholstery thread. (outside view)

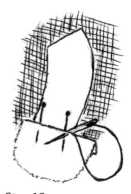

**Step 18**

Step 18: Pin Paw fabric to Inside Arm as shown, and sew with regular weight thread. Repeat this step with other Inside Arm. (outside view)

Step 19: Pin Inside Arm to Outside Arm piece, and sew with upholstery thread. (outside view) Repeat for other arm. Lightly stuff arms so they lie against the body.

**Step 19**

Step 20: Pin arms to Body, checking that they are placed properly; then sew with upholstery thread. (outside view)

**Step 20**

Step 21: Sew head to body using upholstery thread. (You may find it difficult to pin the head to the body first. In that case, just place it as best you can, and deeply stitch the head to the body.) (outside view)

**Step 21**

Step 22: Tie a ribbon around the neck, add some lace, a hat, spectacles, whatever you like!

**Step 22**

Fred Abear, designed and hooked by Judy Taylor, 10" tall, hand-spun yarn on burlap

Ta da! Enjoy your wonderful creation!

Welcome Home Rug, 32"x17" designed and hooked by Judy Taylor, wool and mohair yarns on linen

# Chapter 6

# Project #2
# Dutch Treat

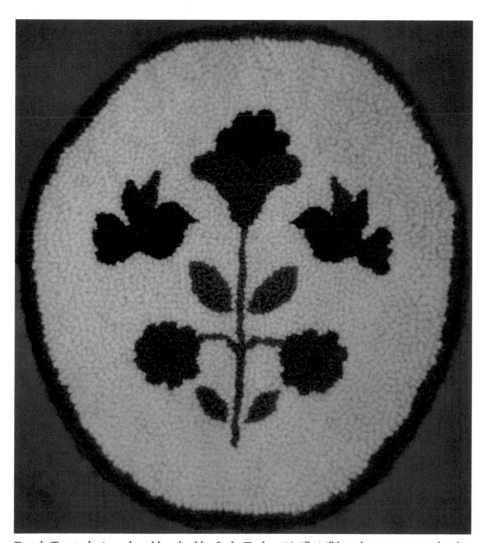

Dutch Treat, designed and hooked by Judy Taylor, 13.5"x16" handspun yarn on burlap

Let's experiment with detail in your second project. One thing that I've learned about rug hooking is that no two hookers will hook the project in the same way. Not only do we differ in the colors that we choose, but we also interpret designs differently. In a design like this one, it really doesn't matter how you interpret the design (your birds may be larger than the ones pictured here, or your flowers smaller, etc). Try to make one bird look like the opposite one--unless you're not fond of symmetry, in your world, in which case, let whatever flutters your wings be your guide! For this project you will need:

Rug hook
Scissors
Sharpie Pen
Fiberglass window screen
½ yd. burlap
3 oz white yarn
2 oz gold yarn
2 oz red yarn
½ oz green yarn

HOOKING DUTCH TREAT

Transfer the pattern onto window screen, and then lay it on the middle of the burlap, and trace over all the lines again with the Sharpie pen. You should go over all the lines on the burlap again when you remove the window screen.

Every once in a while look at the work, both from the top and the underside. On top, you should not be able to see the backing; the yarn should fill in the space as it spreads out on the top. The piece should lie pretty flat when you take it off the frame. On the back, you should be able to see the backing. If you can't see any backing on the underside, you are probably over-packing your loops (see Chapter 3).

I would start hooking this project with the outside border, so that I could hook inside the border without worrying whether the outlines are right. Then I'd do the details next, (such as the stem, leaves, flowers, etc) because you should remember that once you hook near your lines on the burlap, you can't see the lines anymore. Get the details the way you want them first, then you can surround them with background.

If you are using a frame, you might find it more con-
78

Figure 1

venient to put the burlap on your lap to outline the project. I often hook continuous lines or details like this in my lap, because it is so much easier to move the backing around and get the lines just right. Remember to start your outside row one thread inside the line, so your beginning tail will be surrounded when you have finished the hooking.

One great thing about hooking with yarn is that you can easily switch from using a frame to hooking in your lap. I find this really useful, because a frame is great for hooking at home or in my shop or booth, but if I want to hook at a meeting or someplace where I'm going to be sitting for a while, I just leave the frame at home. I can just throw my rug in a bag, and anywhere I can sit down, I can hook.

Hemming the mat:

When you finish the hooking, you can practice doing a simple hem, one that won't have to undergo much wear and tear. Since this project is a wall hanging or a table mat, a simple hem will work just great.

Cut away the extra burlap around the hooked piece, leaving around 3" for your hem. (Figure 1) Since the edges of this mat are rounded, you will need to gather the hem along the fold line, to avoid bulky wrinkles in back when you stitch the hem. To gather the backing for a rounded hem, baste with a needle and thread along the fold line. Carefully pull the thread tight, so the backing pulls together and lays flat against the back of the mat. (Figure 2)

Figure 2

Fold the rest of the burlap under, and pin the area that you've gathered; then baste another section, pull it tight, and pin the rest under. Just be careful that you don't pull the basting thread too tight. Keep adjusting as you go so everything lies flat.

Once you've basted and pinned the whole edge down, you can hem, taking deep stitches so you are sure you are sewing through the backing, and not through a loop of yarn. The idea with a hem like this is not to make the stitches invisible in the back. In fact, if this were a floor rug, you wouldn't want to make the stitches too hard to find because someone might need to repair the rug in the future.

With a steam iron, on the back side of the mat, press the edges of the piece so the hem lies flat. Hey, you did it! Well done, you!

Rooster Mat, 13.5"x16" designed and hooked by Judy Taylor, wool yarn on burlap

Angry Tree, designed and
hooked by Andrea Rheinlander,
16"x26" mixed fibers on linen

# Chapter 7
# Project #3
# Celtic Interlace Mat

Celtic Interlace Mat, 11'x11' designed and hooked by Judy Taylor, Ewenique yarn on burlap

Celtic Pillow, designed by Judy Taylor, hooked by Michele LeBlanc, 12"x12" wool yarn on burlap

Celtic Knot, 48"x52" designed and hooked by Judy Taylor, wool yarn on linen

Celtic Table Runner, 13"x36" designed and hooked by Judy Taylor, wool yarn on linen

In the previous project, Dutch Treat, you had lots of freedom to interpret your design. This Celtic Mat project will increase your skills at detailed work. It really matters with a Celtic interlace that all the lines match up, so you can see the way in which the ribbon pattern seems to go over and under itself.

For this project you will need:

Rug hook
Scissors
Window Screen
Sharpie Pen
Needle and thread
½ yd burlap
2 oz  Outer Background yarn
1 oz Inner Background yarn
2 oz Ribbon yarn
1 oz Ribbon Outline yarn

Use your window screen to transfer the Celtic Mat pattern onto the middle of the burlap. Keep in mind that the lines you have drawn on the burlap disappear when you hook around them, so the best way to hook a Celtic interlace is to do one ribbon at a time, then the one next to it, then the background around them, so you can get rid of the tails sooner, and so that you can be sure that one line really matches the line before it. (Figures 1-3)

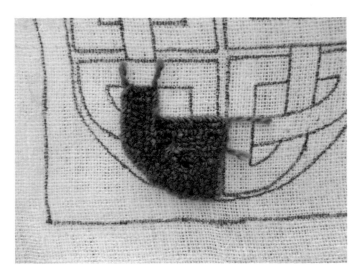

Figure 2

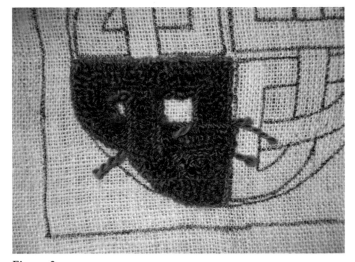

Figure 3

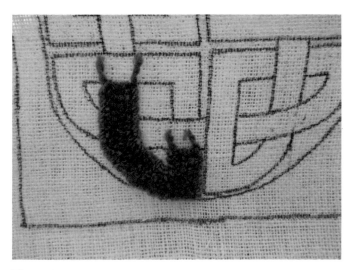

Figure 1

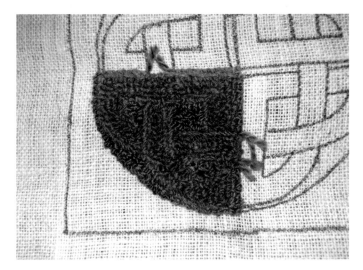

Figure 4

Irish Blessing, 30.5"x22.5" designed and hooked by Judy Taylor, Ewenique yarn on linen

Blessed, 25"x35.5" designed and hooked by Judy Taylor, handspun yarn on linen

In other words, don't try to outline all the ribbons, then fill in the ribbons, then do the background around them. If you start hooking all the ribbon outlines, you will have so many tails in your way, you won't be able to see if the details line up. Much easier to hook one ribbon section at a time, getting rid of those tails as soon as possible. (Figure 4)

When I chose the colors for this mat, I thought they would look nice together, and still appear distinct. However, as I hooked, I noticed that the gold ribbon outline seemed too dull, and the interlace just faded away into the background color. One of the wonderful things about hooking with yarn is how easy it is to "erase" a color and replace it with something else. Turn the rug over, and simply pull out the yarn you want to change. (Figure 5)

Figure 7

Remember, there are no right or wrong colors; just keep trying until you are satisfied. It's your coloring book, after all. I decided to go with the background color (on the right of Figure 7) for my ribbon outline, and pulled out a row of outer background to make a space for me to outline the circle with the ribbon color. Then just for the heck of it, I did a row of ribbon color all around the outside, and another row of the inner background, which gave the mat a nice finished edge.

Figure 5

I tried four different ribbon outline colors (Figure 6), and then narrowed it down to the pink outer background color, and a bright, shiny lilac yarn (Figure 7).

Figure 6

"Oh, I'm sorry, were you using this?"

Celtic Triskellion, 38"x27" designed and hooked by Judy Taylor, wool yarn on linen

Marshall Family Rug, designed and hooked by Linda Rehlinger, 30"x48" handspun yarn and wool strips on burlap

86

When you have finished hooking this project, you will again do a simple hem; but this time you can practice doing a mitered corner to get rid of the bulk in the corners of your mat. Cut away the extra burlap, leaving about 3" for your hem. (Figure 9) Then cut diagonally on each corner, about one inch from each corner. (Figure 10) Fold the diagonal edge down, then fold the edges together, so they meet. (Figures 11 and 12) Pin these down. Then you can fold the rest of the burlap under, and pin down all around the hem. Sew the diagonal folds first, then hem the mat. (Figure 13) Again, you'll want to take deep stitches, making sure you are connecting with the backing, because if you only grab a loop of yarn with your thread, it will just pull out!

Figure 11

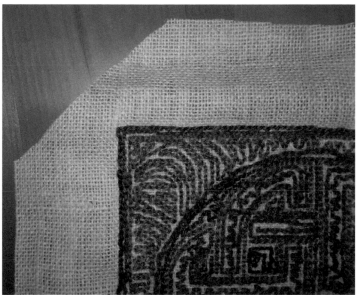

Figure 9

Figure 12

Figure 10

Figure 13

Press the hem on the back with a steam iron. This pattern also makes a nice pillow. You can hand stitch a backing fabric on the mat, and stuff with polyester stuffing. Everyone will be so impressed.

Celtic Love Knot, 48"x52"
designed and hooked by Judy Taylor, wool yarn on linen

The poem in this rug was written by my late brother, Mark Peter Ford, who died when he was eighteen years old. Reprinted here with permission.

*The lover lives in a small world where love is the*
*Moving force..*
*Why tell him life is not as good as it could be?*
*Heartbreak is the only tender hold we have on innocence*
*And if he should never come to the realization*
*    That the universe is heartless, is that a loss?*
*We boast of knowing the "facts of life" but is*
*    It not we who have lost them?*

*The universe would continue to hiss and clank*
*Should love leave it*
*But it is a hopeless task*
*To make him believe it.*

*I will not promise to love forever*
*(Unless man does live forever)*
*But I do promise to love you as long as I am.*

88

# Chapter 8
# Waste Not Want Not

Waste Not Want Not, designed and hooked by Judy Taylor, 31.5"x21.5" wool and mohair yarns on linen

"Waste not, want not," is an adage, or homily, that seems to have been with us since the 16th Century, mainly as a parenting device to urge recalcitrant little munchers to clean their dinner plates if they know what's good for them--answers.com cites this somewhat sterner rendition of the phrase, from a 1576 document: "Willful waste makes woeful want." The phrase was apparently stalwartly applied to the First World War effort in Canada and gained popularity through such propaganda devices as this inspirational home-front gem:

My husband well remembers the phrase from his childhood during World War II, when, as school kids, he and his brother were enlisted (much to their delight) to stomp on and crunch flat every used can, for 'Rosie the Riveter' and her gang to turn into airplanes, tanks and howitzers.

Hooking a rug, wall-hanging or table runner to decorate your home can be a charming, attractive and symbolic way to express personality, family history or character and beliefs.

Teapot Rug, 29"x19" designed and hooked by Judy Taylor, wool yarn on linen

Just a few clever aphorisms that have been hooked into rugs:

> Do as you would be done by.
> Every dog has his day.
> Every Jack has his Jill.
> Faith will move mountains.
> Home is where the heart is.
> Honesty is the best policy.
> Hope springs eternal.
> If life deals you lemons, make lemonade.
> If wishes were horses, beggars would ride.

*If you can't be good, be careful!!*

By now, you will probably have mastered the skill of hooking: you are getting your loops all the same height, with well spaced loops. You've even figured out how to get a nice back side, without any bits of yarn sticking out or any over packing. And so…, it's about time you made your first floor rug!

For this project you will need:

Rug hook
Scissors
½ yard of linen (30"x36")
Window screen
Sharpie Pen
Regular sewing thread and needle
Tapestry needle
Cotton cording 3/16" diameter

8 oz outer background yarn
½ oz lettering yarn
6 oz diamond background yarn
4 oz star yarn
24 oz inner background yarn

HOOKING WASTE NOT WANT NOT

Transfer your pattern to the linen. You will notice that you don't have lots of linen on the sides to wrap around your legs or frame. When hooking on burlap, I don't mind cutting off the leftover on the sides when the project is done and discarding the extra burlap; but linen is much too expensive to waste, so I sew any old fabric on the sides. That way I will always have enough to wrap around my legs, and I can very easily remove the extra fabric when I am ready to do the hem.

The Waste Not Want Not rug is the perfect project for using up leftover yarn bits from other projects. You can also start with new yarn, in any combination of colors that you like. If you happen to have leftovers that you'd like to use, you can hook with them "as is," or you can over-dye them.

Over-dyeing yarn is the easiest type of dyeing, and it is a great way to take leftovers that don't really match and make them look wonderful together. (There are lots of other more complicated dyeing methods that you can use for rug hooking, but I'll cover those in my next book, *Rug Hooker's Guide to the YARNIVERSE*! Stay tuned!)

Take this unattractive bag of leftovers. These yarns were used for different rug hooking projects, as well as knitting and crochet, so they don't really seem to go together at all. However, they are good yarns, and I'm not going to just throw them away. But what can I do with them?

Leftover yarns from other projects

The first thing to do is to get all of the yarn into skeins. To do this I wrap the yarn around a "niddy noddy" and cross-tie the skein three times. This way the yarn won't get tangled in the dye pot, or in the rinsing. If you don't have a niddy noddy, you can wrap the yarn around a chair back, or recruit a friend to hold out his hands so you can wrap the yarn that way.

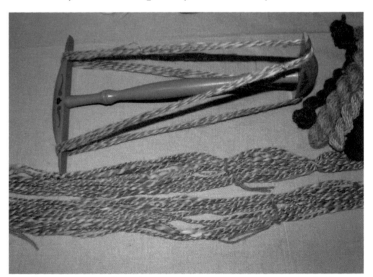

With no particular rhyme or reason, I separated the cross-tied skeins into three piles. I put these piles of yarn into three weak dye baths, one cornflower (light blue), one pine green and one turkey red (Country Classics dyes). You can pick out your own color combination, to match the décor in the room where you'd like the rug to go.

I use large enamel pots for dyeing (the kind you use for canning).

Dyeing procedure:

1. I fill the pot and bring the water to a boil.
2. Then I add a very small amount of the chosen dye color. (Remember: it is always easier to add more dye to the pot than to take it out, so go slow. )
3. Test the strength of the color by dropping a small piece of yarn into the dye. It should take on a hint of the color, but still retain some of the original color. If the effect is not strong enough, you can add a bit more dye at this point.
4. Drop the pile of yarn unceremoniously into the dye bath, and turn the heat down to low.
5. Leave it there for about 20 minutes, then rinse.
6. Fill another large pot with very hot water and a splash of dishwashing liquid, and then transfer the dyed yarn into the soapy pot with tongs.
7. When you have taken out all of the dyed yarn, rinse the first pot and fill it with very hot water.
8. Transfer the skeins to the new pot.
9. Do this one more time, or as long as it takes to rinse out all of the soap. Just make sure that the rinse water is very hot; if you shock the yarn from hot to cold during the rinse, you'll have a felted mess!
10. Throw the dyed skeins into a mesh laundry bag and run them through the "drain and spin" cycle on your washing machine. If your machine doesn't allow you to just run the spin cycle, you can do it the old fashioned way, by "wuzzing." No, I'm not kidding, "wuzzing." Take that laundry bag outside and swing the living tweedle out of it (centrifugal force will spin most of the water out).
11. Then hang the skeins where they can get plenty of air to dry.

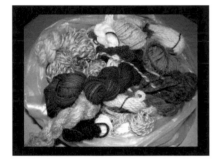
From this.... (yuck)

... to this (yum!)

Wildflower Rug, 48"x24" designed and hooked by Judy Taylor, overdyed wool yarn on linen

Now all of these skeins need to be wrapped back into balls for rug hooking. This is a good job for the volunteer who helped you wrap the skeins. There are a few ways I use to keep my yarns organized while I'm hooking a 'hit-or-miss' project. Sometimes I put balls of yarn into zip lock bags with other like colors. I might have a dark red bag, a light red bag, etc. That helps me to choose what color I want to hook with next, keeps the balls from getting tangled, and it ensures that I'll get to all of them in good time.

TIPS ON HOOKING WASTE NOT

For this project, I separated out my very dark yarns first and set them aside. I hooked the letters, then I hooked the dark background, alternating dark to lighter yarns. (Figure 1) I noticed that I had a substantial amount of yarns that came out turquoise, so I alternated those in continuous rows in the diamond background, and hooked the star with one skein of light blue. (Figure 2)

Figure 1

Figure 2

For the main background, I wanted to make sure I used all of the colors, so I hooked with two large baskets, one on each side of my frame. I would take a color out of the first basket, hook a bit with it, then put that yarn into the second basket. I kept on that way until the first basket was empty, then I went the other way. This was a way of mindlessly assuring that all of those pretty colors got used throughout.

You will notice that the main background in your paper pattern is blank. That's because you get to decide how you want to fill that part up. You can do rows of colors, as I did, or you could do swirls, zig zags, stripes, circles, squares, diamonds--whatever your little heart

desires. How you decide to fill in the area might depend on what yarn you're using. If you're starting with new yarn, you may want to try bold stripes of color, if you have dozens of little bits, then think small, maybe little flowers, etc. Go back to that box of crayons and doodle!

Don't forget to incorporate your initials and the year somewhere in the rug. (Remember that, whenever you hook a woolen rug, you're creating a bit of folk-art history, as well as family history, given the durability and longevity of the product; and fifty years after the fact, you and your grandkids might really enjoy being able to know when and how that piece of fabric art was created!)

When you have finished hooking (yay!), cut the linen so there is about 3" all around the rug. (Figure 3) We will be doing a mitred corner this time, but first we need to bind the edge. We didn't bind the edges of Dutch Treat or the Celtic Mat, because those small projects will not be walked on. If we did that same thing with a floor rug, the linen would eventually break along the edge of the rug, because of repeated walking, washing and general wear and tear. By binding the edge, we prevent the linen from folding flat along the hooked edge, ensuring the rug a long, long life.

Figure 3

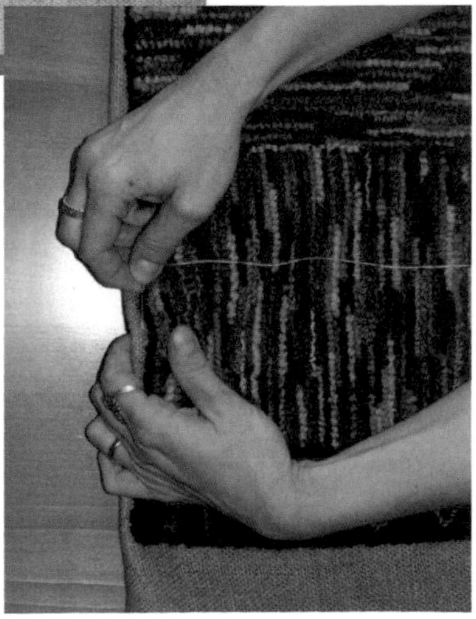

Figure 4

Wrap the linen around the cotton cording, so the edge sticks out beyond the hooked area. With a regular needle and thread, baste the linen around the cord. (Figure 4) When you come to the corner, wrap the extra linen around the cord, taking care to shape the corner so it looks square from the top. (Figure 5)

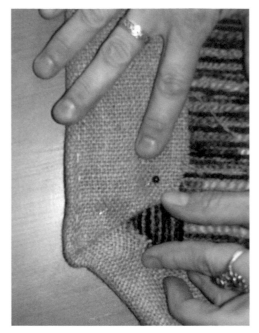

Figure 7

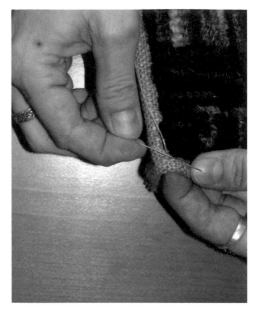

Figure 5

Figure 8

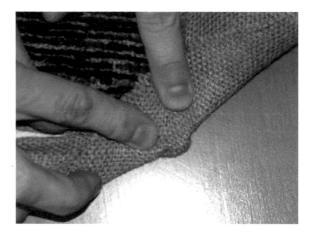

Figure 6

On the back, fold the hem down the middle of the corner (Figure 6). Fold the backing down one side of the corner and pin this part down. (Figure 7) Do the same for the other side of the corner hem, so that the two folds meet diagonally. (Figure 8) Don't worry about pinning down the whole hem at this point--let's do the binding first.

Using a tapestry needle and some matching yarn, you can now bind the edge. First bring your needle up from the back to the front, and leave a small amount of yarn in the back. (Figure 9) Now bring your needle again up from the back to the front, holding the yarn end in your left hand. Keep whip-stitching in this way, sewing over the tail in the back. (Figure 10)

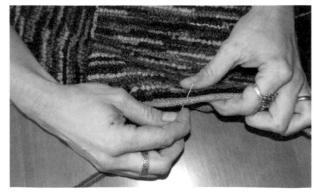

Figure 9

94

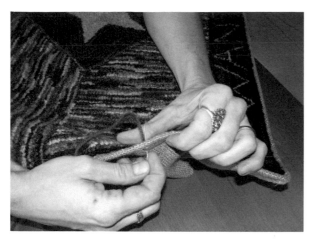

Figure 10

Once you've established your stitching, you need to turn the yarn around, so that your final end will come on the back side of the rug. Push your needle into the front of the rug, and bring it out the back. (Figure 11) Keep stitching until you run out of yarn, leaving a tail sticking out of the back. Thread the needle again, and start from back to front first, sewing over both tails this time. Then turn the yarn around so all the tails end up in the back. Carefully stitch around the corner so all of the linen is covered by yarn. (Figure 12)

Figure 11

Figure 12

When you have whip-stitched all around the edge (you clever thing) push your needle under the stitching in back, so you have your final tail underneath the stitching. Cut the tail so the end disappears in the back. (Figure 13)

Figure 13

Fold your linen edges under for your hem, and pin in place. With regular needle and thread, hem the rug, making sure you are taking deep stitches, connecting to the backing, not to just a bit of yarn. You should also stitch up the diagonal folds in the corners. (Figure 14)

Figure 14

Press your hem on the back side of the rug with a steam iron.

Congratulations on fulfilling a lifelong dream. Now you are a hooker.

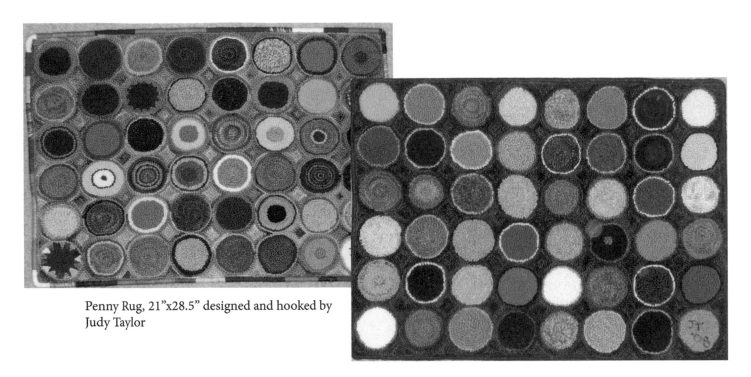

Penny Rug, 21"x28.5" designed and hooked by
Judy Taylor

Crown of Thorns, 36"x22" designed and
hooked by Judy Taylor, wool yarn on linen

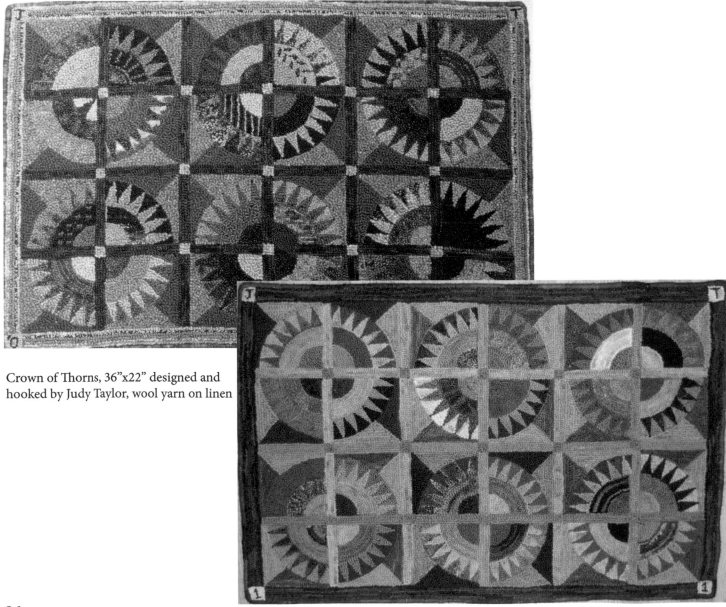

# Chapter 9

# Making your own spiffy rug hooking frame

Hooking on a standing frame

Slip in the shorter legs, and it becomes a lap frame

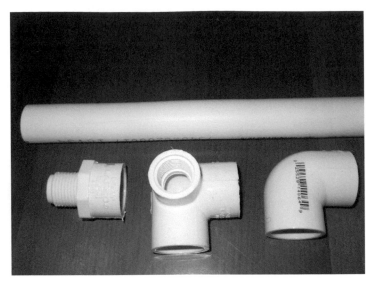

To frame or not to frame? Of course, it is a matter of personal preference. You may really dig rug hooking, but don't like wrapping the backing around your legs. This is a real consideration if you plan to do any rug hooking in the summertime (how would you like wrapping yourself in 3 lbs. of wool during a heat wave?). A frame also allows you to shift your position, which can be helpful if you plan to hook for a few hours at a time.

I developed this frame with the help of many students. While I've come up with a design that works for most everyone, the nice thing about making your own frame is that you can customize it to suit your style and individual needs.

You will need:

2-10' long, ¾" PVC pipe, lightweight (200 PSI)

PVC plumbing fittings:
6 elbows with side outlet socket x FIPT, ¾"x½"
6 adapters, male MIPT x socket, ½"x¾"
2 elbows 90 degrees, ¾"

Rubber cupboard material
Goop adhesive
2-4 Large clamps

Cut your PVC pipes into the following lengths:

**A** 4-8.5"
**B** 3-16.5"
**C** 2-23.5"
**D** 2-22"
**E** 2-4"
**F** 2-2.5"

Letter guide to other pieces:

**G** elbow with side outlet socket x FIPT, ¾'x½'
**H** adapter, male MIPT x socket, ½"x ¾"
**I** elbow, 90 degrees, ¾"

I wash all the pieces at this point, because PVC can be pretty grimy when you get it from the hardware store.

I recommend that you fit all the pieces together without gluing first, to check for any pieces that you might want longer, shorter, etc. This is your chance to customize your frame. So follow the instructions to assemble your frame without glue, then if you decide you would like the legs longer or shorter, or the frame wider or narrower, you can make those adjustments before you do your final assembly.

ASSEMBLY INSTRUCTIONS:

Top section:

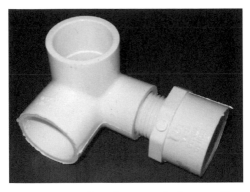

Screw in male adapters (**H**) into elbows with side outlet (**G**). You do not need to glue this connection (**G-H** connection).

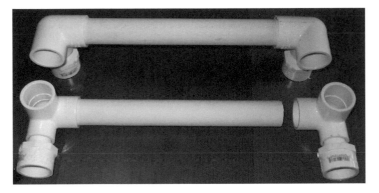

Glue one of the (**A**-8.5" pipes) into (**G**) on both ends. Repeat for the other (**A**-8.5" pipe) of top section so that the **G-H** connections face toward one another and are the same length.

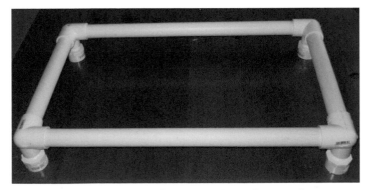

Glue two of the (**B** 16.5") into (**G**) as shown above. Make sure the unit is square and lies flat when you put it on a table--all four corners should sit solidly on a flat table. (Note: check the flatness of the piece immediately upon putting together, so that you can make necessary adjustments--if it doesn't lie flat--before the glue sets.)

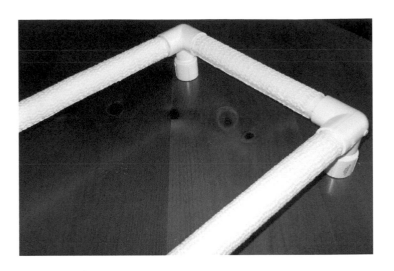

Cut two pieces of rubberized material 3.5"x7". Glue these on the outside of (**A**- 8.5" pipes). Cut two pieces of rubberized material 3.5"x15" and glue these on the outside of (**B**- 16.5" pipes).

Le Chat Noir, adapted and hooked by Judy Taylor, 15.5"x21" commercial yarn on linen

Bottom section:

Glue the third (**B**-16.5") into the remaining two (**G-H**) connections.

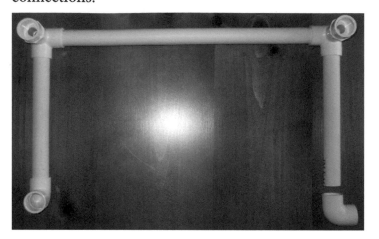

Glue the two remaining (**A** 8.5") into (**G**) as shown below. Glue (**I** elbow, 90 degrees) into other end of (**A**) with outlet pointing upwards (same direction as **H**).

Check all the glued sections to make sure everything is square. The nice thing about using Goop for this job is that it does not dry instantly, so you can adjust things as you go to get a good square frame. The glue should allow for some tweaking for 15-20 minutes or so. Then it will be dry enough to use in about 24 hours.

What you have left now are two sets of legs, one for the standing frame and one for the lap frame. To set up the standing frame, push both (**C**) 23.5" pipes into (**I**) in the bottom section, and push the two (**D**) 22" pipes into (**H**). Then you can push the top section down on the legs. Don't glue these ones though; you will want to switch easily from standing frame to lap frame, so the legs always slip on and off. If you want to set up the lap frame, push the (**E**) 4" pipes into (**I**) on the bottom section, and push the (**F**) 2.5" pipes into (**H**). Then push the top section down on the legs, just as you did with the standing frame.

To use your frame, lay your backing, pattern side up, on the top section of the frame. Use your clamps to connect the backing snugly around the outside of the frame. If you wish, you can also put an extra set of clamps on the other two rubberized pipes, but it is not necessary.

When not in use, your frame collapses so you can carry it in a totebag!

# Chapter 10

# Yarn Hooking--
# Past, Present and
# Future

Smiling Horse, 61"x37" ca. late 19th Century, wool yarn.  Courtesy of Linda Rosen Antiques

An exciting new museum project is on the horizon which will be solely devoted to rug hooking. The Hooked Rug Museum of North America has been the dream of Suzanne and Hugh Conrod of Chester, Nova Scotia, who saw the heritage and history of this craft fading away, and so began to collect artifacts and supporters to assist in the dream of an entire museum dedicated to the history and artistry of this uniquely North American craft.

The museum, which is scheduled to open in 2012 will feature rug patterns and pattern-making equipment from the Garrett factory in 19th Century Nova Scotia as well documents and patterns from early designers and collectors Philena Moxley, Ralph Burnham and Edward Sands Frost, dating as far back as the mid-1800's, and a rare copy of the first correspondence course in rug hooking history, written by 20th century teacher and artist, Pearl McGown. Other museum highlights will be brochures, advertisements, letters, and all sorts of documents which trace the history of this humble craft. Never before has there been a whole museum devoted to the rich heritage of rug hooking, and I for one cannot wait to visit!

Welcome Cat rug, 34"x19" wool yarn. Courtesy of Chris Searfoss

The board for the museum has been hard at work research-ing every artifact, rescuing precious items from dusty attics and moldy, cobwebbed basements, fundraising, and educating the public on the history of rug hooking in North America. They have done some innovative projects to promote rug hooking, such as an event called "At Grand-mother's Knee," where senior citizens in Nova Scotia, rang-ing from 65-93, paired up with beginning rug hookers to share the craft with a new generation. Some of the seniors in the project hooked replicas of the museum's rare patterns, and in all 50 replicas and 52 "My First Rugs" made by the participants were donated to the museum. "At Grandmother's Knee" was such a success that other areas are starting their own projects to encourage seniors to share their talents and skills.

Cat with Kittens, 61"x32" ca. late 19th Century, wool yarn. Courtesy of Linda Rosen Antiques

102

"Hands Across the Border" is another such museum project, where rare patterns were replicated with the help of expert hookers from many areas of the United States . Along with these rugs, the museum will have many antique examples of rug hooking, including rugs hooked with yarn in the Cheticamp style, a 50 sq. ft. rug hooked with hemp on a hemp background, Grenfell rugs from the 1920's hooked with nylons, and many other treasures detailing the regional styles of rug hooking in North America.

Crystal Morash and Yvonne MacLean, Participants of "At Grandmother's Knee." Courtesy of the Hooked Rug Museum

Beginning in 2011, they will open a shop on the premises, which will educate and inspire the public to appreciate this craft. Patterns, books and hand-hooked rugs will be available for sale, which will help to fund the opening of the museum. The precise opening date of the museum will depend on the donations received. The sooner they raise the necessary funds, the sooner we can all enjoy this fantastic museum (hint, hint).

As soon as the "brick and mortar" phase is complete, and the museum is open to the public, the goal is to create a web presence for the museum, where all of its archives will be available to the public in a "virtual museum." Visitors to the website will be able to research the history of rug hooking, and share the rug hooking stories from their own lives. If a trip to Chester, Nova Scotia is not a possibility for you, the museum will be as close as your own computer.

I am truly grateful to the Conrods, and the hundreds of dedicated volunteers they have inspired, for making the dream of a rug hooking museum a reality.

Mid-20th Century floral, 23"x40" wool yarn on burlap

Old Farm Rug, 26"x50" ca. mid-20th Century, wool yarn. Courtesy of Anthony Onorato, Flowerdew Antiques

"Our major challenge has been to inspire all organized rug hooking groups in Canada and the United States to rally around our efforts to create the first museum, gallery and archives of rug hooking in North America. Generous publicity, kind words, respected advice, concerns, suggestions and challenges have come from numerous sources at every level from grass-roots to the upper echelons. We have had a major communication challenge to spread our gospel over the massive space of two nations. However, the seeds have been solidly planted and there have been "helping hands" at every turn.

Like all of us in the widespread sisterhood of rug hookers, we have long been saddened to see our history melting away before our eyes, our heritage disappearing in the busy world around us; and instead of being able to share space in the beautiful museums and galleries of the art world, we have been relegated to community halls and church basements. It is a void we are determined to fill." Suzanne Conrod

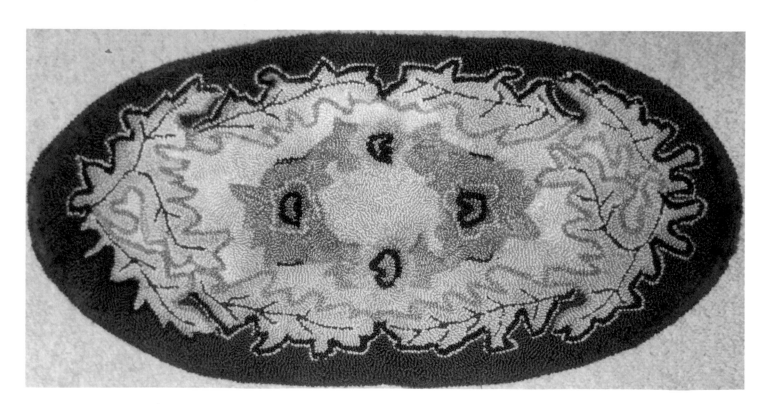

Priscilla Turner Rug, 1930's, 23"x48" wool yarn on cotton

*If Old Rugs Could Speak-- What Stories They Would Tell*
*(Copyright the Hooked Rug Museum of North America Society, excerpted here with permission)*

Hooking wool yarns and other hand-cut and spun materials into a loom-woven foundation was initiated for utilitarian purposes in unique American techniques by our continent's earliest settlers. Making do with the minimal materials available to them, they created bed coverings (rugs) and floor coverings (mats) to warm the modest and drafty log cabins which they called home. Few examples of this early art form have survived. Spun wool from sheep was available at an early date, but it is evident that some of the earliest hooked artifacts were grown from seed! (A major research document-- Rug Art "Grown From Seed" is now being compiled by HRMNA based on major new discoveries and by professional qualified assessment of fabrics.)

Earliest North American hand hooking of utilitarian items evolved within the geographic boundaries of old Acadia (northern New England and the Maritime provinces) possibly dating back to the earliest planting of seeds and agricultural development at Port Royal in 1607. Both hemp and flax were available home-grown materials, while natural dyes from barks, berries and vegetable sources provided color. Patterns were primitive, drawn with pointed sticks burned at the tip to create a charcoal tracing pencil for marking out the homespun material.

Floral Rug, hooked by Mabel Brooks, 1945

Heritage, designed and hooked by Bonnie Campbell, commercial and sweater yarn on linen

As settlement in the continent evolved, so did the art and its substance. A number of corn husk rugs, for example, have been discovered in New Brunswick (King's Landing Museum, New Brunswick).

Evidence also exists that spun yarns were on occasion created from cat-tails, sometimes called bull rushes. Several such have been found and sold privately by a Riverview, New Brunswick, antique dealer. The growing of sheep throughout pioneer settlements also led to an ongoing harvest of wool which to this day still remains in constant demand for rug making. Eventually, cotton materials became available from the continent's southern areas, and, even later, synthetic materials contributed to rug making's evolution. Social change and the industrial age brought about great changes for the early craft as it grew rapidly from, in the mid 1800's, the advent of imported burlap feed bags for use as rug hooking foundation, through the post- second world war period. At its contemporary level as a fine art tapestry, sometimes referred to as "painting with wool," yarn types utilized range the gamut from synthetics to both plant and animal hair fibers.

While the first priority in rug making was strictly utilitarian, its evolvement as an art form began at a very early date. The Museum's research teams have found a number of what they suspect are very early hemp based rugs. These unique items have been discovered in a variety of older homes in south western Nova Scotia communities, the Anapolis Valley and Colchester County regions as well as in the Miramichi area of New Brunswick. Conflicting opinions as to probable material content have necessitated retention of a qualified conservator to undertake microscopic examination of the fibers to assure accuracy. Such research results were being conducted at this writing.

The hooked items found which contained the still unconfirmed plant fibers are also important because they are mostly unique in their primitive designs as well as materials used. It is now apparent they will fill another, little known void in early rug hooking history. How far back they date may never be determined. Their images are a flash-back to pre-pattern days depicting the robins of spring, resting on branches of pussy willows, farm animals, and interestingly, one which depicts two fishermen guiding their fishing schooner through rocky shoals to their anchorage.

One of them has been identified as a "casket rug," possibly the first of its kind ever found in Canada. Biblical symbols, including a bible and cross as well as flowers are depicted in its long, narrow design. It is primarily a yarn hooked rug and the yarn component appears to be a plant rather than wool fiber. Casket rugs are also known in New England but are still considered a rarity there. Apparently they were used in northern areas as a replacement for the traditional wreath of flowers placed on coffins which were unavailable during winter months. The Nova Scotia rug was discovered in the attic portion of a remodeled building that was once used as a block house in Chester (built in the late 1700's) to ward off raids from the sea by privateers. Another of the plant fiber rugs discovered in a more than century-old home in Lunenburg County, Nova Scotia, is also of a twine type of yarn and like others of its vintage and material is of a naïve primitive design which is a probable indication that it too was created prior to availability of commercial patterns. Some include scrolls, geometric and floral shapes, copied from household furniture and pottery. Innovation was alive and well, even at an early stage of rug art creation.

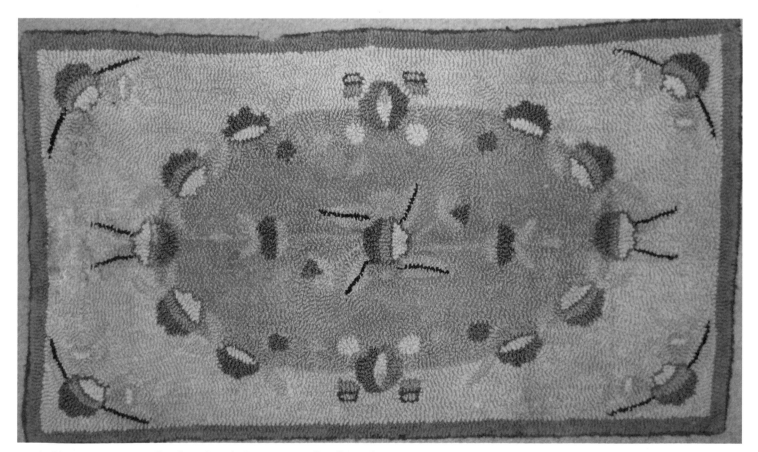

A charming primitive floral, mid-20th Century, 34.5"x57" wool yarn on cotton

Mable Bell, wife of the late Alexander Graham Bell led the effort to create a rug hooking industry in the struggling fishing community of Cheticamp, which still thrives today and provides sustenance for entire families who once depended on the now hard-hit fishery for survival. This industry was based on wool yarn mostly in fine single and double strands. A distinctive material used by the rug hookers of this area to create their hooked artifacts to this day.

Rug hooking in all its myriad forms continues to flourish today throughout the continent, but its heritage has been slighted. Literally, the craft turned art has been "tramped on" for too long and the rug hooking community at large has, as a result, rallied around a movement to create the first Museum, Gallery and Archives in the world in the Hubbards/Queensland region of Nova Scotia, a region which has always been a hotbed of rug making. In one year alone, more than 23,000 hand hooked rugs were shipped for sale from the maritime provinces to markets in Boston and New York. The Chester-Aspotogan area near the future Museum's location was described in a 1920's newspaper article as the maritime centre for this production.

Antique Dollhouse Rug, probably punch hooked, 8.5"x15" silk yarn on cotton

Reindeer Rug, ca. 1940, 34"x21" wool yarn on cotton, courtesy of Susan Ingram, A Rustic Garden

Pair of old rugs, mid-20th Century, each measures 21"x32" wool yarn on cotton

Antique "Wire Hair Fox Terrier" rug, 23"x39" yarn on cotton

Flower Rug, 33.5"x24.5" designed and hooked by Judy Taylor, handspun and commercial yarn on linen

CPSIA information can be obtained
at www.ICGtesting.com
Printed in the USA
LVIC010002260113
317197LV00003B

* 9 7 8 0 6 1 5 5 1 4 6 5 9 *